CONTENTS

Unit 4: Christmas

Unit 5: God Formed His Nation

Unit 6: The Wilderness

Unit 4: CHRISTMAS

Big Picture QUESTIONS

Session 1: What part did Mary and Joseph have in God's plan? God chose Mary and Joseph to be the earthly parents of Jesus.

Session 2: Why was Jesus born? Jesus was born to be God's promise Savior.

Session 3: Why did the wise men visit Jesus? The wise men came to worship Jesus as King.

Unit 4: CHRISTMAS

Unit Description: God's plan for the redemption and salvation of His people is brought to earth through the person of Jesus Christ. Christmas is the time we choose to celebrate Jesus' birth on earth.

Unit Key Passage: Luke 2:10-11

Unit Christ Connection: The Savior God had promised was born!

Session 1: Angels Spoke to Mary and Joseph
Luke 1:26-56; Matthew 1:18-24

Session 2: Jesus Was Born
Luke 2:1-20

Session 3: Wise Men Visited Jesus
Matthew 2:1-21

Teacher BIBLE STUDY

People had been waiting a long time for Jesus. God hinted at His coming in the garden of Eden when He promised a seed to conquer the serpent. (Gen. 3:15) The prophets told of His coming hundreds of years before His birth. God was working out His plan to bring His people back to Himself.

In the Bible, God used angels to communicate His message to people. Angels spoke to Abraham in Genesis 18. The Angel of the LORD spoke to Balaam in Numbers 22. Now Mary and Joseph, the earthly parents of Jesus, each received a special visit from an angel to announce the birth of God's promised Messiah. The angel Gabriel's announcement to Mary surprised her. By His grace, God chose Mary to be the mother of His child. The angel's message revealed much about this promised child.

First, He would be great in both being and nature. He would be the Son of the Most High. Jesus is the Son of God, and the Lord God promised to give Him the throne of His father David. These words fulfilled the prophecy given to David in 2 Samuel 7:12-16. He would reign over the house of Jacob forever. His kingdom would have no end.

The good news that Jesus was coming into the world was good news because of why He was coming. An angel revealed Jesus' purpose to Joseph in Matthew 1:21: "He will save His people from their sins." The gospel is the good news of what God has done for us through Christ.

The announcement of Jesus' birth is not the beginning of the gospel; God had been planning for this moment since before the beginning of time. (See Eph. 1:3-10.) Help the kids you teach understand that God's plan has always been to save sinners and bring them back to Himself. Jesus, whose name means "Yahweh saves," is the culmination of that plan.

Younger Kids BIBLE STUDY OVERVIEW

Session Title: Angels Spoke to Mary and Joseph
Bible Passage: Luke 1:26-56; Matthew 1:18-24
Big Picture Question: What part did Mary and Joseph have in God's plan? God chose Mary and Joseph to be the earthly parents of Jesus.
Key Passage: Luke 2:10-11
Unit Christ Connection: The Savior God had promised was born!

Small Group Opening

Large Group Leader

Small Group Leader

The BIBLE STORY

Angels Spoke to Mary and Joseph
Luke 1:26-56; Matthew 1:18-24

One day God sent an angel named Gabriel to a town in Galilee called Nazareth. The angel went to visit a young virgin named Mary. She was engaged to be married to Joseph, a descendant of King David.

The angel said to Mary, "Rejoice! You have found favor with God. He is with you." Mary was very afraid and puzzled. Why would God find favor with her? She had done nothing special.

The angel told Mary to not be afraid. He told Mary that she was going to have a very special and unique baby, and they would call the baby Jesus, which means "the LORD saves." The angel explained that the baby would be great—He would be God's Son! He would even be a king—the King God had promised would come.

Mary asked the angel, "How can that happen? I am not married yet."

The angel replied, "God will be the father of the baby. The baby will be God's Son."

The angel Gabriel told Mary, "Nothing will be impossible with God!" He told Mary that her relative Elizabeth was pregnant, even though she was old and did not have any children.

Mary replied, "I belong to God. May everything happen just as you said." Then the angel left her.

Mary hurried to her relative Elizabeth's house. When she arrived, the baby inside Elizabeth leaped for joy! The Holy Spirit filled Elizabeth and she said, "What an honor, Mary! Your baby will be blessed too!"

Mary was so happy. She praised God with a song about how great God is. Mary knew every family in the future would say she was blessed because God was going to do great things for her through Jesus. God was keeping His promise to bless the whole world through Jesus.

Mary stayed with Elizabeth for three months. Then she went home.

Now Joseph found out Mary was going to have a baby, but Joseph knew it was not his baby—Mary and Joseph were not married yet! Joseph decided to quietly divorce Mary so she would not be publicly disgraced.

Soon after Joseph thought these things, an angel appeared to him in a dream.

"Joseph!" the angel said. "Don't be afraid to take Mary as your wife, because the baby she is carrying was put there by the Holy Spirit. Mary is going to have a son; name Him Jesus because He is going to save His people from their sins!"

This happened just like the prophet said it would: "See, the virgin will become pregnant and give birth to a son, and they will name Him Immanuel," which is translated "God with us."

When Joseph woke up, he did exactly as the angel commanded. He married Mary, and when she had a son, Joseph named Him Jesus.

Christ Connection: "Therefore, the Lord Himself will give you a sign: The virgin will conceive, have a son, and name him Immanuel" (Isaiah 7:14). The baby Jesus fulfilled Isaiah's prophecy, as well as other prophecies of the coming Savior throughout the Old Testament. Through His life, death, and resurrection, Jesus fulfilled God's plan of redemption that God planned from the beginning of the world.

Small Group OPENING

Session Title: Angels Spoke to Mary and Joseph
Bible Passage: Luke 1:26-56; Matthew 1:18-24
Big Picture Question: What part did Mary and Joseph have in God's plan? God chose Mary and Joseph to be the earthly parents of Jesus.
Key Passage: Luke 2:10-11
Unit Christ Connection: The Savior God had promised was born!

Welcome time

Arriving Activity: Jumping for Joy

Encourage the kids to individually share something they really want for Christmas. Repeat what each child wants, and invite the other kids to jump for joy if they would like that gift, too.

Say • There is a Christmas gift that everyone should jump for joy to receive. We will find out what gift in today's lesson.

Activity page (5 minutes)

• "Best Gift" activity page, 1 per kid
• pencils

Guide boys and girls to complete the activity page.

Say • Christmas is an exciting time as we celebrate the day God sent His only Son to earth.

Session starter (10 minutes)

Option 1: Chosen

Choose two to four kids based on something they have in common. Suggestions include eye color, gender, type of clothing, color of clothing, names start with the same letter, and so forth. Invite the kids to guess why they were chosen.

Say • It feels good to be chosen. In today's Bible story, God chose two people for a very special purpose.

- "Countdown Calendar," 1 per kid (enhanced CD)
- construction paper, 1 per kid
- crayons or markers

Option 2: Countdown calendar

Invite the kids to color and decorate the Christmas countdown calendar included with this session. Encourage the kids to glue the calendar to a piece of construction paper for stability.

Say • In today's Bible story, God used angels to tell Joseph and Mary about Jesus. Today, God wants us to deliver that message to others. From now until Christmas, try to think about someone you can tell about Jesus. Write that person's name on the line for one of the days.

Transition to large group

Large Group LEADER

Session Title: Angels Spoke to Mary and Joseph
Bible Passage: Luke 1:26-56; Matthew 1:18-24
Big Picture Question: What part did Mary and Joseph have in God's plan? God chose Mary and Joseph to be the earthly parents of Jesus.
Key Passage: Luke 2:10-11
Unit Christ Connection: The Savior God had promised was born!

- room decorations
Tip: Don't be afraid to place Christmas trees in the middle of the desert or Christmas lights around your lush river valley archaeology site.

Suggested Theme Decoration Ideas: Use any traditional Christmas decorations that are appropriate for your church environment. If you are pausing in the middle of another theme to celebrate Christmas, decorate the theme you have with Christmas decorations.

Countdown

- countdown video

Show the countdown video as your kids arrive, and set it to end as large group time begins.

Introduce the session (1 minute)

- piece of paper

[Large group leader enters carrying a piece of paper with a list on it.]

Leader • I just love Christmas. I enjoy the food, the smells, the decorations. What else is there? Of course, the presents. How many of you make a list of the things you want for Christmas? Me, too! I have my list right here. A list is the way we communicate or tell others what we really, really want under the tree. Have you ever wondered how Mary and Joseph knew they were going to have Jesus? How would they know He would be much more than an average baby?

Timeline map (1 minute)

Leader • I'm sure our timeline map has the answer we are looking for. Up until now, we have been traveling through the Bible in the order that events actually happened. However, we couldn't just keep going and skip Christmas. After all, Christmas is a great day of the year! So, let's fast forward hundreds of years. Here's the answer about how Mary and Joseph knew about Jesus. It's the title of today's Bible story, "Angels Spoke to Mary and Joseph." In today's story, we will find out what the angels said and how they shared the big news with the couple.

Big picture question (1 minute)

Leader • I have another question that needs to be answered. It's our big picture question. What do we always need to answer the big picture question? That's right, the Bible. The Bible tells us about God's plan to save us and how we should live out His plan.

If you have your Bible, please hold it up high in the air. The Bible shares the message that the angels delivered to Mary and Joseph. They would have a big part in God's plan. That brings us to our big picture question. ***What part did Mary and Joseph have in God's plan?***

Sing (5 minutes)

Leader • Do you know God's plan for Jesus? He was born as our Savior. He was born so that we might have life. That reminds me of a song—our theme song. Let's sing and praise God for the greatest Christmas gift of all. Sing together "Born That We May Have Life."

• Timeline Map

Tip: Hang the panel with the Christmas unit on the wall some distance from the current panels. If you have the entire timeline map on the wall, hang a star above the panel with Christmas.

• "Born That We May Have Life" song

Key passage (4 minutes)

- "He Was Born" song
- Key Passage Slide or Poster (enhanced CD)

Leader • Angels didn't just speak to Mary and Joseph about the birth of Jesus. They told a group of shepherds taking care of their flocks where to find Baby Jesus. Their announcement is our key passage for the next few weeks.
Show the slide or poster of this unit's key passage, Luke 2:10-11. Lead the boys and girls to read the verse together.

Leader • This message was originally shared with the shepherds, but it remains good news for us today. Let's put these verses to music as a reminder that we can celebrate His birth, too.
Sing together "He Was Born."

Tell the Bible story (10 minutes)

- "Angels Spoke to Mary and Joseph" video
- Bibles, 1 per kid
- Bible Story Picture Slide or Poster (enhanced CD)

Leader • Why don't we see if we can find out the answer to our big picture question. Find Luke 1 in your Bibles. *What part did Mary and Joseph have in God's plan?*
Choose to tell the Bible story in your own words using the script provided, or show the "Angels Spoke to Mary and Joseph" video.

Leader • The angel Gabriel told Mary she would have a baby, but not just any baby. He would be God's Son. Gabriel told Mary that her relative, Elizabeth, was pregnant, too. Mary was so excited she went to visit Elizabeth and sang praises to God. Meanwhile, Joseph decided not to be with Mary anymore once he found out Mary was pregnant, and it wasn't his baby. An angel told him it was OK because God was the baby's father. The angel told him Jesus would be born to save people from their sins. *What part did Mary and Joseph have in God's plan? God chose Mary and Joseph to be the earthly parents of Jesus.*

Ask the following review questions:

1. What did Gabriel first tell Mary? (*to rejoice because God had chosen her and was with her, Luke 1:28*)
2. What did the angel tell Mary she would have? (*a baby, Luke 1:31*)
3. What did Elizabeth's baby do when Mary greeted her? (*leaped, Luke 1:44*)
4. When did Joseph change his mind about leaving Mary? (*after a dream where an angel visited him, Matthew 1:20,24*)
5. What prophet said Jesus would be called Immanuel? (*Isaiah; Isaiah 7:14*)

Discussion starter video (3 minutes)

• "Missing Player" video

Leader • Everyone has a part in God's plan. Think about that as we watch this video.

Play "Missing Player."

Leader • Would you ever play a soccer game without a goalie? All the parts of a team are important. God has a plan for you just as he had a plan for Mary and Joseph. ***What part did Mary and Joseph have in God's plan? God chose Mary and Joseph to be the earthly parents of Jesus.*** The first step in seeking God's plan for your life is to repent and trust Jesus. God's plans for us are centered around His Son Jesus. God wanted His people to know that a Savior was coming. God's plan from the beginning of time was to send Jesus to save us from our sin.

The Gospel: God's Plan for Me (optional)

Use Scripture and the guide provided with this session to explain to boys and girls how to become a Christian. Assign individuals to meet with kids who have more questions. If this is not possible, encourage boys and girls to ask their parents, small group leaders, and other Christian adults any questions they may have about becoming a Christian.

• Big Picture Question Slide or Poster (enhanced CD)

Prayer (5 minutes)

Leader • Alright, let's take a few minutes to remember what we learned today.

Show the big picture question slide or poster.

Leader • Does anyone know the answer to our big picture question? *What part did Mary and Joseph have in God's plan? God chose Mary and Joseph to be the earthly parents of Jesus.*

Ask the kids to choose their favorite Christmas color, red or green. Those who choose red will ask the big picture question, and those who choose green will answer. Swap roles and repeat.

Before transitioning to small group, make any necessary announcements. Lead the kids in prayer. Pray that your kids will understand that God has a plan for their lives and they must seek Jesus to find it.

Dismiss to small groups

The Gospel: God's Plan for Me

Ask kids if they have ever heard the word *gospel*. Clarify that the word *gospel* means "good news." It is the message about Christ, the kingdom of God, and salvation. Use the following guide to share the gospel with kids.

God rules. Explain to kids that the Bible tells us God created everything, and He is in charge of everything. Invite a volunteer to read Genesis 1:1 from the Bible. Read Revelation 4:11 or Colossians 1:16-17 aloud and explain what these verses mean.

We sinned. Tell kids that since the time of Adam and Eve, everyone has chosen to disobey God (Romans 3:23). The Bible calls this sin. Because God is holy, God cannot be around sin. Sin separates us from God and deserves God's punishment of death (Romans 6:23).

God provided. Choose a child to read John 3:16 aloud. Say that God sent His Son Jesus, the perfect solution to our sin problem, to rescue us from the punishment we deserve. It's something we, as sinners, could never earn on our own. Jesus alone saves us. Read and explain Ephesians 2:8-9.

Jesus gives. Share with kids that Jesus lived a perfect life, died on the cross for our sins, and rose again. Because Jesus gave up His life for us, we can be welcomed into God's family for eternity. This is the best gift ever! Read Romans 5:8; 2 Corinthians 5:21; or 1 Peter 3:18.

We respond. Tell kids that they can respond to Jesus. Read Romans 10:9-10,13. Review these aspects of our response: Believe in your heart that Jesus alone saves you through what He's already done on the cross. Repent, turning from self and sin to Jesus. Tell God and others that your faith is in Jesus.

Offer to talk with any child who is interested in responding to Jesus.

Small Group LEADER

Session Title: Angels Spoke to Mary and Joseph
Bible Passage: Luke 1:26-56; Matthew 1:18-24
Big Picture Question: What part did Mary and Joseph have in God's plan? God chose Mary and Joseph to be the earthly parents of Jesus.
Key Passage: Luke 2:10-11
Unit Christ Connection: The Savior God had promised was born!

- Key Passage Slide or Poster (enhanced CD)
- dry erase board and markers (optional)

Key passage activity (5 minutes)

Make sure the key passage, Luke 2:10-11, is visible for each child, either as the printed poster or written on a dry erase board. Read the verse together.

Say • Just as an angel told Mary and Joseph that they would be the earthly parents of Jesus, an angel shared the birth of Jesus with shepherds watching their sheep. The angel told them Jesus' birth would be great joy for all people. That's still true today. We can celebrate because of the joy Jesus brings to those who know and love Him.

Remind the kids that the angel appeared to Joseph in a dream. Ask what we are usually doing when we dream (*sleeping*). Read through the key passage several times together. Invite the kids to close their eyes as if sleeping and say the first few words together. Instruct them to look again and finish the passage. Encourage the kids to close their eyes during different parts of the passage.

- Bibles, 1 per kid
- Small Group Visual Pack
- Big Picture Question Slide or Poster (enhanced CD)

Bible story review (10 minutes)

Encourage the kids to find Luke 1 in their Bibles. Help them as needed.

Say • Where in the Bible is the story of Jesus' actual birth found, Old Testament or New Testament? (*New Testament*) The Christmas story is found in a part of the New Testament we call Gospels. The Gospels are made up of four books. Does anyone know what those books are? (*Matthew, Mark, Luke, John*) The events leading to Jesus' birth and those shortly after are found in Matthew and Luke.

Use the small group visual pack to show kids where today's Bible story is on the timeline. Review the Bible story provided or summarize the story in your own words. Encourage the kids to listen to the following statements an angel made to either Mary or Joseph. If the kids think the angel was talking to Mary, they should hold their arms like they are rocking a baby. If they think it was the angel speaking to Joseph, they should pillow their head in their hands and pretend to be sleeping. The statements are below.

1. Don't be afraid because God has chosen you. (*Mary*)
2. God will give Jesus a throne and He will be King forever. (*Mary*)
3. Jesus will save people from their sins. (*Joseph*)
4. Your relative, Elizabeth, is also pregnant. (*Mary*)
5. They will call the baby Immanuel. (*Joseph*)
6. Jesus will be called the Son of God. (*Mary*)

Say • An angel spoke to Mary and Joseph, making it clear that Jesus was no ordinary baby. Each angel also made sure Mary and Joseph understood they had a very important part in Jesus' birth.

Show the big picture question slide or poster.

Say • That brings us to our big picture question and answer. ***What part did Mary and Joseph have in God's plan? God chose Mary and Joseph to be the***

earthly parents of Jesus. From the beginning of time, God planned to send Jesus to save us from sin. That's the message the angels had for Mary and Joseph. It's the same message the Bible has for us.

Activity choice (10 minutes)

Option 1: Joy leaping

Group the kids into pairs. The pairs face each other. Designate one kid in each pair as "same" and the other as "opposite." Instruct the kids to jump straight up four times together. Count together as they jump. On the fifth jump, each kid should come down with one foot in front of the other. If they come down with the same leg out, the kid designated "same" is the winner. If they come down with opposite legs out, the kid designated "opposite" wins. Swap partners and play again.

Say • The baby inside Elizabeth leaped for joy when Mary came near. He didn't leap because of Mary, but because of Baby Jesus. Mary and Joseph were given special parts in God's plan. *What part did Mary and Joseph have in God's plan? God chose Mary and Joseph to be the earthly parents of Jesus.*

- chenille stems, 1 per kid
- jingle bells, 1 or more per kid
- hymnal

Option 2: Praise bells

Provide each child with one chenille stem and one or more small jingle bells. Fold the chenille stem in half. Demonstrate how to weave the folded chenille stem through the handle of the bells. Sing a carol or any Christmas song, and allow the kids to play their bells.

Say • Mary praised God because He chose her to be Jesus' mother. She had a special part in God's plan to save His people.

• What part did Mary and Joseph have in God's plan? God chose Mary and Joseph to be the earthly parents of Jesus.

- folder, 1 per kid
- Journal Page, 1 per kid (enhanced CD)
- markers or crayons
- Bible Story Coloring Page

Journal and prayer (5 minutes)

Distribute each child's journal and the journal page provided with this session. Instruct the kids to draw the angel talking to either Mary or Joseph. Kids who are able to write can write the key passage below their picture.

Say • What is our big picture question and answer for today? *What part did Mary and Joseph have in God's plan? God chose Mary and Joseph to be the earthly parents of Jesus.*

Tip: Each quarter the *Younger Kids Activity Pack* includes a set of *Big Picture Cards for Families*. Don't forget to give the card pack to parents today to allow families to interact with the biblical content each week.

Make sure each child puts this week's sheet in his journal and then collect them. Keep the journals in the classroom so they will be available every week or as often as you wish to use them.

If time remains, take prayer requests or allow kids to complete the coloring sheet provided with this session. End the session with prayer, thanking God for sending His Son to save us from our sins. Pray for each child by name, and thank God for His plan for each one.

Teacher BIBLE STUDY

God is in control of all things. Do you think it was just by chance that Caesar Augustus called for a census? Did it just so happen that Mary and Joseph were traveling to Bethlehem—the very place the Messiah was prophesied to be born? (Micah 5:2) God used a pagan emperor to bring about His plan.

God's plan was for Jesus to be born in a manger. A king born in a manger! It was so unlikely. But Jesus was no ordinary baby. He was God's Son, sent in the most humble of circumstances, "not to be served, but to serve, and to give His life—a ransom for many" (Matthew 20:28).

Imagine the shepherds' surprise when an angel of the Lord suddenly appeared. The Bible says that they were terrified! But the angel said to them, "Don't be afraid, for look, I proclaim to you good news of great joy that will be for all the people: Today a Savior, who is Messiah the Lord, was born for you in the city of David" (Luke 2:10-11).

What a relief! This angel had come to bring good news. First, he proclaimed a Savior. The people of Israel were well aware of their need for a Savior. They made sacrifices daily to atone for their sin. Finally, a Savior had come who would be the perfect sacrifice for sin, once and for all. Jesus was also Messiah the Lord. The word *Messiah* means "anointed one," especially a king. The Deliverer and Redeemer would be King over His people. And this was all happening in Bethlehem, the city of David—just as the prophet Micah said.

This is the best news ever! An army of angels appeared, praising God and saying: "Glory to God in the highest heaven, and peace on earth to people He favors" (Luke 2:14). The purpose of Jesus' birth was twofold: to bring glory to God and to make peace between God and those who trusted in Jesus' death and resurrection to provide salvation.

Younger Kids BIBLE STUDY OVERVIEW

Session Title: Jesus Was Born
Bible Passage: Luke 2:1-20
Big Picture Question: Why was Jesus born? Jesus was born to be God's promised Savior.
Key Passage: Luke 2:10-11
Unit Christ Connection: The Savior God had promised was born!

Small Group Opening

Large Group Leader

Small Group Leader

The BIBLE STORY

Jesus Was Born
Luke 2:1-20

During the time Mary was pregnant with Baby Jesus, the Roman emperor, Caesar Augustus, announced that everyone needed to be registered for a census. Every person traveled to the town where his family was from. Since Joseph was a descendant of King David, he and Mary left Nazareth and traveled to Bethlehem, the city of David.

While they were there, the time came for Mary to have her baby. Mary and Joseph looked for a safe place for Mary to have her baby, but every place was full because of all the people who were in town to be counted. So Mary and Joseph found a place where animals were kept, and that is where Mary had her baby, Jesus. She wrapped him snugly in cloth, and she laid him in a feeding trough, where the animals ate their food.

In the same region, some shepherds were staying out in the fields and watching their sheep to protect them from thieves and predators. All of a sudden, an angel of the Lord stood before them. A bright light shone around the shepherds, and they were terrified!

But the angel said to them, "Don't be afraid! I have very good news for you: Today a Savior, who is Messiah the Lord, was born for you in the city of David." Then the angel said, "You will find a baby wrapped snugly in cloth and lying in a feeding trough." A king in a feeding trough? That was no place for a king!

All of a sudden, a whole army of angels appeared, singing to God and saying, "Glory to God in the highest heaven, and peace on earth to people He favors!"

So the shepherds went straight to Bethlehem to find Baby Jesus. They found Mary and Joseph, and the baby who was lying in the feeding trough. The shepherds went and told others about the baby Jesus. Everyone who heard about Jesus was surprised and amazed. Mary thought about everything that was happening and tried to understand it. The shepherds returned to their fields, praising God because everything had happened just as the angel had said.

Christ Connection: The birth of Jesus was good news! Jesus was not an ordinary baby. He was God's Son, sent to earth from heaven. Jesus came into the world to save people from their sins and to be their King.

Small Group OPENING

Session Title: Jesus Was Born
Bible Passage: Luke 2:1-20
Big Picture Question: Why was Jesus born? Jesus was born to be God's promised Savior.
Key Passage: Luke 2:10-11
Unit Christ Connection: The Savior God had promised was born!

Welcome time

Arriving Activity: Christmas chat

Kids love to talk about Christmas. Engage the kids in conversation as they enter the room. Possible questions are listed below.

Say • What do you like most about Christmas?
• What is Christmas Day like at your house?
• Where are the places you celebrate Christmas?
• When do you get to open presents?

Activity page (5 minutes)

• "Light the Way" activity page, 1 per kid
• pencils

Guide boys and girls to complete the activity page.

Say • An angel told the shepherds about the birth of Jesus. The shepherds were so excited that they hurried to go see Him for themselves. Today, we will get to hear why they hurried to see Him and praised God all the way home.

Session starter (10 minutes)

Option 1: I decree

Explain that a decree is like a law. It must be followed. Decrees were common during Jesus' time, issued by the Roman Emperor. Tell the kids that you will play the role of an emperor, and you will issue decrees they must follow.

However, they may only do the actions with "I decree" before them. Decrees may be broad like "jump up and down" or targeted like "boys find someone with blue eyes and give them a high-five." If a child breaks a decree or does an action that has not been decreed, he must stand against the wall. After a few commands, issue a decree that allows the kids on the wall to rejoin.

Say • Today's Bible story talks about a decree from a pagan emperor. God used this decree to fulfill part of His plan to send Jesus at just the right place and time.

Option 2: Shepherd watching

- non-spring clothespin, 1 per kid
- markers
- chenille stem, 1 per kid
- candy cane, 1 per kid

Tip: The candy cane will have to be adjusted until the shepherd is balanced.

Provide each child with a non-spring clothespin. Encourage the kids to turn the clothespin into a person by making the top of the clothespin the head, the middle part the body, and the bottom part the legs. Invite them to color on a face and clothes. Distribute the chenille stem and a small individually wrapped candy cane. Demonstrate how to wrap the chenille stem around the body, creating a belt and arms with one arm a little longer than the other. Instruct each child on how to wrap the end of the longer arm around the candy cane, creating a staff.

Say • The first people to hear that Jesus had been born were shepherds. We'll find out today how they found out and what they did when they heard about His birth.

Transition to large group

Large Group LEADER

Session Title: Jesus Was Born
Bible Passage: Luke 2:1-20
Big Picture Question: Why was Jesus born? Jesus was born to be God's promised Savior.
Key Passage: Luke 2:10-11
Unit Christ Connection: The Savior God had promised was born!

• countdown video

Countdown

Show the countdown video as your kids arrive, and set it to end as large group time begins.

• baby doll

Introduce the session (1 minute)

[Large group leader enters carrying a baby doll wrapped in a blanket. Whisper as if the baby is asleep.]

Leader • Only a few things are more exciting than a baby's birth. How many of you have a younger brother or sister? Do you remember the day they were born? Have any of you seen pictures or videos of your own birth? When a baby is born, people get excited. They take pictures. They want to hold the baby. They make a big deal every time the baby smiles or even opens his eyes. Well, today we get to hear about the birth of a baby that should make us all excited. This baby's birth was in an unusual place, and some unusual people came to visit. This baby was very special.

• Timeline Map

Timeline map (1 minute)

Leader • I bet we can find a picture of this baby's birth, too. Let's look at our timeline. Remember, we skipped ahead last week to where we were studying in our Bible because we wanted to celebrate Christmas together. Last week we found that an angel told Mary and Joseph that they would be Jesus' earthly parents. Here is our picture of Mary, Joseph, and a little baby. This special baby is Jesus.

Big picture question (1 minute)

Leader • Let's see those Bibles. It's exciting to have your very own Bible. If you have your Bible, please hold it up so we can see it. These are God's words, written so we can learn about Jesus and come to know and love Him.

The Bible you hold in your hands is full of verses that tell us about Jesus. He is the main character. We learn about Him before His birth, during His life, and after His death and resurrection. Have you ever wondered why Jesus left heaven to become a baby? That brings us to our big picture question for today. *Why was Jesus born?*

Sing (5 minutes)

• "Born That We May Have Life" song

Leader • Why would God want to send His Son to a place so full of sin? Sin separated all people from God. People had no way to have a relationship with God. They had no hope, but all of that changed because God had a plan. Let's praise Him for His plan to bring Jesus to save people from their sin.

Sing together "Born That We May Have Life."

Key passage (4 minutes)

• "He Was Born" song
• Key Passage Slide or Poster (enhanced CD)

Leader • If you knew God's Son was going to be born in your town, who would you invite to celebrate? You might think about family, friends, or important people. God's plan was different. No kings or governors were invited; God invited a group of shepherds.

Show the slide or poster of the key passage, Luke 2:10-11. Lead the boys and girls to read the verses together.

Leader • The good news of Jesus' birth was not just for the famous, the powerful, or the rich; it was for all kinds of people. That's what the two verses we just read tell us. Our key passage song will help us remember them.

Sing together "He Was Born."

Tell the Bible story (10 minutes)

• "Jesus Was Born" video
• Bibles, 1 per kid
• Bible Story Picture Slide or Poster (enhanced CD)

Leader • Let's look in our Bibles and find out why Jesus came to earth as a baby. Find Luke 2 in your Bibles.

Choose to tell the Bible story in your own words using the script provided, or show the "Jesus Was Born" video.

Leader • Joseph and Mary went to Bethlehem because the emperor wanted to get a count of all the people. They couldn't find a place to stay, so Jesus was born in a place where animals were kept. Then, an angel visited some shepherds that were close by. The angel told them a baby had been born who would be their Savior. The shepherds went and worshiped Baby Jesus. After that, they went and told everyone. ***Why was Jesus born? Jesus was born to be God's promised Savior.***

Ask the following review questions:

1. What city was Jesus born in? (*Bethlehem, Luke 2:4-6*)
2. Joseph went to Bethlehem to be part of a census because of which relative? (*David, Luke 2:4*)
3. Where did Mary and Joseph place Jesus after his birth? (*a manger or feeding trough, Luke 2:7*)
4. Who did the angels tell of Jesus' birth? (*shepherds, Luke 2:8-10*)
5. ***Why was Jesus born? Jesus was born to be God's promised Savior.*** (*Luke 2:11*)

Discussion starter video (4 minutes)

Leader • Have you ever thought about how you celebrate Christmas? Is it something like this?

Play "Deck the Halls."

Leader • The kids were all talking about things and ways they celebrate Christmas. Did they leave out anything important? They forgot the most important thing about Christmas. It's when we celebrate Jesus' birth! *Why was Jesus born? Jesus was born to be God's promised Savior.*

While the presents, decorations, and time with family are all great things, the real reason we celebrate is because Jesus, our Savior, was born. He lived perfectly and He gave us the best gift of all. Jesus sacrificed His own life to take the punishment we deserve for our sin. He became our Savior.

The Gospel: God's Plan for Me (optional)

Use Scripture and the guide provided with this session to explain to boys and girls how to become a Christian. Assign individuals to meet with kids who have more questions. If this is not possible, encourage boys and girls to ask their parents, small group leaders, and other Christian adults any questions they may have about becoming a Christian.

Prayer (4 minutes)

• Big Picture Question Slide or Poster (enhanced CD)

Show the big picture question slide or poster.

Leader • Before we move on, did anyone hear the answer to our big picture question? *Why was Jesus born? Jesus was born to be God's promised Savior.*

Ask the kids to choose whether they like Christmas cookies or candy canes. Direct those who choose cookies to ask the big picture question and those who choose candy canes to answer. Swap roles and repeat.

Before transitioning to small group, make any necessary announcements. Lead the kids in prayer. Pray that kids will understand that Jesus came as our Savior, and we should always celebrate His birth, His life, His death, and His resurrection for us.

Dismiss to small groups

The Gospel: God's Plan for Me

Ask kids if they have ever heard the word *gospel*. Clarify that the word *gospel* means "good news." It is the message about Christ, the kingdom of God, and salvation. Use the following guide to share the gospel with kids.

God rules. Explain to kids that the Bible tells us God created everything, and He is in charge of everything. Invite a volunteer to read Genesis 1:1 from the Bible. Read Revelation 4:11 or Colossians 1:16-17 aloud and explain what these verses mean.

We sinned. Tell kids that since the time of Adam and Eve, everyone has chosen to disobey God (Romans 3:23). The Bible calls this sin. Because God is holy, God cannot be around sin. Sin separates us from God and deserves God's punishment of death (Romans 6:23).

God provided. Choose a child to read John 3:16 aloud. Say that God sent His Son Jesus, the perfect solution to our sin problem, to rescue us from the punishment we deserve. It's something we, as sinners, could never earn on our own. Jesus alone saves us. Read and explain Ephesians 2:8-9.

Jesus gives. Share with kids that Jesus lived a perfect life, died on the cross for our sins, and rose again. Because Jesus gave up His life for us, we can be welcomed into God's family for eternity. This is the best gift ever! Read Romans 5:8; 2 Corinthians 5:21; or 1 Peter 3:18.

We respond. Tell kids that they can respond to Jesus. Read Romans 10:9-10,13. Review these aspects of our response: Believe in your heart that Jesus alone saves you through what He's already done on the cross. Repent, turning from self and sin to Jesus. Tell God and others that your faith is in Jesus.

Offer to talk with any child who is interested in responding to Jesus.

Small Group LEADER

Session Title: Jesus Was Born
Bible Passage: Luke 2:1-20
Big Picture Question: Why was Jesus born? Jesus was born to be God's promised Savior.
Key Passage: Luke 2:10-11
Unit Christ Connection: The Savior God had promised was born!

- Key Passage Slide or Poster (enhanced CD)
- dry erase board and markers (optional)
- candy canes, 3 or 4

Key passage activity (5 minutes)

Make sure the key passage, Luke 2:10-11, is visible for each child, either as the printed poster or written on a dry erase board. Read the verses together.

Say • What a message the angels delivered to the shepherds! The angels told them a Savior was born. God had promised the Israelites that a Savior would rescue them. We find this all throughout the Old Testament. They may not have understood exactly what that Savior would do or look like, but they knew He was supposed to come. *Why was Jesus born? Jesus was born to be God's promised Savior.* He came and gave His life so we could be forgiven for our sins. Jesus is our Savior as much as He was the Savior of those shepherds.

Read the verse a few times together to become familiar with it. Invite the kids to form a circle and hold out a pointer finger from either hand as if pointing at someone. Place a candy cane on a kid's finger. After that kid says the first word of the key passage, she is to pass the candy cane to the next kid in the circle by allowing it to slide from her finger onto his finger. No one is allowed to touch the candy cane with any other body part. Once the pass is made, the next kid is to say the second word. Continue until the key passage is complete. If someone drops the candy cane, invite him to pick it up and continue. Provide extras in case one breaks.

Bible story review (10 minutes)

• Bibles, 1 per kid
• Small Group Visual Pack
• Big Picture Question Slide or Poster (enhanced CD)

Encourage the kids to find Luke 2 in their Bibles. Help them as needed.

Say • Luke 2 is where we find the story of Jesus' birth we hear the most. What other book tells us about Jesus' birth? (*Matthew*) These books are part of the four New Testament books called what? (*Gospels*) What do the Gospels tell us? (*about Jesus' life and ministry on earth*)

Use the small group visual pack to show kids where today's Bible story is on the timeline. Review the Bible story provided or summarize the story in your own words. Encourage the kids to act out the Bible story as you read it from Scripture. Before you start, select someone to be Joseph and someone to be Mary. Choose some of the kids to be shepherds and some to be angels. Choose one person to be Caesar Augustus. Each child should get a part. Designate one part of the room as the place Jesus was born and another part as a field for the sheep. As you read about each person or group, tell the kids to go to the part of the room where they belong and act out their parts. Pause as you read to remind the kids of what they should do next.

Say • You have all just acted out one of the greatest events in history.

Show the big picture question slide or poster.

Say • Don't forget our big picture question and answer. ***Why was Jesus born? Jesus was born to be God's promised Savior.*** Now you know why we celebrate

Christmas. God's promised Savior was born to save sinners.

Activity choice (10 minutes)

Option 1: Long way

Tape two or more lines at one end of the room and a matching number of lines at the other end, making sure no obstacles are between them. Explain that the start line is Nazareth and the finish line is Bethlehem. Place the kids into groups based on the number of start and finish lines. Instruct each group to line up single file behind one of the start lines. Encourage the first kids in line to race each other from Nazareth to Bethlehem. Instead of allowing the kids to run, give instructions on how they must get to Bethlehem. Invite them to hop, skip, crawl, and so forth. Vary your instructions as each set of kids races each other. Continue as time allows.

• tape

Say • Mary and Joseph had to travel 70 miles from Nazareth to Bethlehem while Mary was pregnant. Traveling would not have been easy. They had no cars, no planes, and no buses. They had to walk all that way or use an animal to carry them. It was no accident they had to travel all that way because Micah 5:2 said a ruler over Israel would come from Bethlehem.

Option 2: Wreath craft

• chenille stems, 1 green and 2 red per kid
• heavyweight paper, 1 per kid (optional)
• glue (optional)

Provide each child with one green chenille stem and two red chenille stems. Twist a red and green stem together. Twist the two ends together to form a circle. Take the other red chenille stem and fold each end over the middle, making a bow. Twist the ends between the two loops over the middle of the stem, so the bow stays together. Attach the bow to the

Tip: Glue the
finished wreath
on the front of
a folded piece
of construction
paper or piece of
heavyweight paper
to make a Christmas
card.

wreath by twisting the two loose ends of the bow under and
back over the bottom of the wreath. Encourage the kids to
hang the wreath on their door or Christmas tree.

Say • The wreath forms a never-ending circle. The message
of Jesus is never-ending, too. He will forever be our
Savior because He came and lived the perfect life,
died, and rose again. *Why was Jesus born? Jesus
was born to be God's promised Savior.*

Journal and prayer (5 minutes)

- folder, 1 per kid
- Journal Page, 1 per
  kid (enhanced CD)
- markers or crayons
- Bible Story Coloring
  Page

Distribute each child's journal and the journal page
provided with this session. Instruct the kids to draw a
manger with Baby Jesus. Encourage kids who can write to
write *King and Savior* below the picture.

Say • Can someone tell us our big picture question and
answer one more time? *Why was Jesus born? Jesus
was born to be God's promised Savior.*

Make sure each child puts this week's sheet in his journal
and then collect them. Keep the journals in the classroom so
they will be available every week or as often as you wish to
use them.

If time remains, take prayer requests or allow kids to
complete the coloring page provided with this session. End
the session with prayer, thanking God for sending Jesus as
our Savior. Pray for each child by name, and ask God to
help each child to focus on Jesus this Christmas.

Teacher BIBLE STUDY

The wise men were *magi*. Their study of the stars led them to Judea to find and worship Jesus, the newborn King. Before they found Jesus, though, the wise men met King Herod. God had promised the Jewish people a new king—one who would save them from their enemies. King Herod was not that king. Imagine how he felt when he heard about a new king in town.

The wise men asked him, "Where is He who has been born King of the Jews?" The wise men unintentionally challenged Herod's reign. Not only was Herod not a full Jew, he was not a descendant of King David. Herod was deeply disturbed by the news that this child had the birthright of being king.

Herod was furious. He gathered his chief priests and scribes to determine where Jesus had been born. Then he lied to the wise men: "When you find Him, report back to me so that I too can go and worship Him." What deceitfulness! The truth was, Herod did not want to worship Jesus at all; he wanted to kill Him!

The wise men continued on their journey and found Jesus. They worshiped Him. The Bible does not say how many magi worshiped Jesus, although they brought Him three gifts—gold, frankincense, and myrrh. Jesus may have been about two years old when the magi found Him. The wise men were warned in a dream to avoid Herod, so they returned home by another route.

The wise men came to worship Jesus as King. Jesus is the King who will rule forever, as God promised to King David in 2 Samuel 7. Help the children you teach realize that Jesus is the true King who is worthy of all our worship.

Younger Kids BIBLE STUDY OVERVIEW

Session Title: Wise Men Visited Jesus

Bible Passage: Matthew 2:1-21

Big Picture Question: Why did the wise men visit Jesus? The wise men came to worship Jesus as King.

Key Passage: Luke 2:10-11

Unit Christ Connection: The Savior God had promised was born!

Small Group Opening

Large Group Leader

Small Group Leader

The BIBLE STORY

Wise Men Visited Jesus
Matthew 2:1-21

A long time ago, God promised the Jewish people that He would send a king to save them from their enemies. The people were still waiting for their King, but the time had finally come. Jesus was born in Bethlehem of Judea at the same time Herod was king. Was Herod the king God promised? No! Herod was an evil king.

God sent a star to show the wise men that Jesus had been born. The wise men traveled to find Him. They came to King Herod. "Where is the king of the Jews?" they asked. "We saw His star in the east and have come to worship Him."

A new king? Herod was king! King Herod was very angry. He assembled all the chief priests and scribes. They looked at what the prophets had written to figure out where Jesus had been born.

"And you, Bethlehem, in the land of Judah, are by no means least among the leader of Judah: because out of you will come a leader who will shepherd My people Israel," the chief priests and scribes quoted the prophet Micah.

Herod took the wise men aside. He asked them when the star appeared. Then he spoke to them in private. "Go and search carefully for the child. When you find Him, report back to me so that I too can go and worship Him." But Herod was lying. He didn't want to worship the new king; he wanted to kill Him!

The wise men followed the star until it led them to Jesus. When they saw the star, they were filled with joy! The wise men went into the house where Jesus was with His mother, Mary. They fell to their knees and worshiped Jesus. Then they gave Jesus gifts: gold, frankincense, and myrrh. When it was time for the wise men to go home, God warned them in a dream not to tell Herod where Jesus was. So they took a different way home.

After the wise men were gone, an angel appeared to Joseph, Mary's husband, in a dream. The angel said, "Get up! Take the child and His mother, flee to Egypt, and stay there until I tell you. For Herod is about to search for the child to destroy Him."

Younger Kids Bible Study Leader Guide
Unit 4 • Session 3

So in the middle of the night, Joseph got up and took Mary and Jesus to Egypt where they would be safe.

King Herod was so mad! The wise men didn't tell him where Jesus was! He was so angry that he killed all the boys in Bethlehem under two years old. He wanted to make sure he killed Jesus, but he didn't know Jesus had escaped.

A while later when Herod died, an angel spoke to Joseph again in a dream. "Get up! Take the child and His mother and go to the land of Israel, because those who sought the child's life are dead." So Joseph did what the angel said. He got up and took Mary and Jesus to the land of Israel.

Christ Connection: The wise men came to worship Jesus as King. Jesus is the King who will rule forever, as God promised to King David in 2 Samuel 7. Jesus is the true King who is worthy of all our worship.

Small Group OPENING

Session Title: Wise Men Visited Jesus
Bible Passage: Matthew 2:1-21
Big Picture Question: Why did the wise men visit Jesus? The wise men came to worship Jesus as King.
Key Passage: Luke 2:10-11
Unit Christ Connection: The Savior God had promised was born!

• star stickers or star ornament

Welcome time
Arriving Activity: Star finders
Before class begins, hide star stickers throughout the room or tell kids to close their eyes while you hide and re-hide a star ornament.
Say • Today we will study a group of men who looked for a star after the greatest birth in all of history.

• "Star Moment" activity page, 1 per kid
• pencils

Activity page (5 minutes)
Guide boys and girls to complete the activity page.
Say • The wise men came to worship Jesus as King. Today, we will talk about how Jesus deserves our worship.

Session starter (10 minutes)
Option 1: Get up
Choose two to four volunteers to come to the front of the room. Invite all the kids still seated to bow their heads and close their eyes. Explain that they are "sleeping," and they may not wake up until they hear "get up." Each volunteer should tap the shoulder of someone sleeping. Instruct the sleepers to raise their hands when they get tapped on the shoulder, but they may not open their eyes. The volunteers should come back to the front of the room after each has

tapped someone on the shoulder. The leader will then say "get up." The sleepers wake up, and those who were tapped on the shoulder try to guess who chose them.

Say • Imagine an angel waking you up and telling you to get up and flee. That happened to Mary and Joseph in today's Bible story.

Option 2: Star cracker

- graham cracker, 1 per kid
- white or yellow frosting
- plastic knife, 1 per kid

Provide a graham cracker for each child. Demonstrate how to break the cracker down the middle seam to form two squares. Instruct the kids to use a plastic knife to spread a small layer of frosting on one of the crackers. Turn the unfrosted cracker slightly and lay it on top of the frosted side of the other cracker. The two crackers should be stuck together forming an eight-point star. Add more frosting until the crackers are covered.

Say • Imagine following a star to the place where Jesus was born. That's how God led the wise men to where young Jesus was.

Transition to large group

Large Group LEADER

Session Title: Wise Men Visited Jesus
Bible Passage: Matthew 2:1-21
Big Picture Question: Why did the wise men visit Jesus? The wise men came to worship Jesus as King.
Key Passage: Luke 2:10-11
Unit Christ Connection: The Savior God had promised was born!

• countdown video

Countdown

Show the countdown video as your kids arrive, and set it to end as large group time begins.

Introduce the session (1 minute)

• crown

Tip: If you don't have a crown available to you, use a piece of construction paper to make one.

[Large group leader enters wearing a crown.]
Leader • Who would like to be a king or queen? Not too many kings or queens still rule in the world today, but during Bible times it was very common. What would you do if you were a royal ruler for a day? When Jesus was born, shepherds came to worship Him as Savior. Some time later, another group of people came to worship Him as King. Today we will learn about this group and how they found Jesus.

Timeline map (1 minute)

• Timeline Map

Leader • This is our last week to talk about Christmas. Next week we will go back to where we left our timeline in the Old Testament. Let's look at what we have discovered about the birth of Jesus. Just a few weeks ago, we saw how an angel told Mary and Joseph that they would be the earthly parents of Jesus. Last week we got to see Jesus' birth and how He was born as the Savior promised by God. We are about to find out who came to worship Jesus days, months, or maybe even a year or more after His birth.

Big picture question (1 minute)

Leader • It's time to see if you brought your Bible. Hold your Bible up. Inside your Bible are many stories about God's plan to rescue His people from sin through Jesus. In one story, a group of wise men came to see Jesus as a child. That brings us to our big picture question. *Why did the wise men visit Jesus?*

Sing (5 minutes)

• "Born That We May Have Life" song

Leader • Many people realized how important Jesus was even as a baby. Mary and Joseph, shepherds, and angels celebrated this baby boy who would change the world. The wise men were no different. They had waited and watched for His birth. We get to see the whole picture. We can worship Jesus, knowing He was born so that we may have eternal life.

Sing together "Born That We May Have Life."

Key passage (4 minutes)

• "He Was Born"
• Key Passage Slide or Poster (enhanced CD)

Leader • An angel sent an invitation to a group of shepherds to come see the promised Savior. The angel told them Jesus' birth was good news for everyone.

Show the slide or poster of this unit's key passage, Luke 2:10-11. Lead the boys and girls to read the verses together.

Leader • Even as this message was delivered to the shepherds, another invitation was being sent to another group of men. This invitation was through a special star that appeared after Jesus' birth.

Sing together "He Was Born."

- "Wise Men Visited Jesus" video
- Bibles, 1 per kid
- Bible Story Picture Slide or Poster (enhanced CD)

Tell the Bible story (10 minutes)

Leader • *Why did the wise men visit Jesus?* Let's find out. Find Matthew 2 in your Bibles.

Choose to tell the Bible story in your own words using the script provided, or show the "Wise Men Visited Jesus" video.

Leader • The wise men followed a star that led them to where Jesus was. *Why did the wise men visit Jesus? The wise men came to worship Jesus as King.* Herod was the king of that area, so he was angry when the wise men told him they were seeking a child who would be King. He tried to trick them, but God knew Herod's plans.

After the wise men visited Jesus and worshiped Him, God led them home another way. Then, an angel told Joseph to get up and go to Egypt because Herod wanted to kill Jesus. When Herod died, Jesus and His family came back to Israel.

Ask the following review questions:

1. Who did the wise men tell Herod they were looking for? (*King of the Jews, Matthew 2:2*)
2. What did the wise men follow to get to Jesus? (*a star, Matthew 2:2,9*)
3. What three gifts did the wise men give to Jesus? (*gold, frankincense, and myrrh; Matthew 2:11*)
4. Why did an angel tell Joseph to take Mary and Jesus and leave for Egypt? (*Herod was angry and wanted to kill Jesus, Matthew 2:13*)
5. *Why did the wise men visit Jesus? The wise men came to worship Jesus as King.*

Discussion starter video (5 minutes)

Leader • The wise men traveled many miles to worship Jesus as King. Do you ever complain about going just a few miles to church, or do you understand how important worshiping Jesus is?

Play "Worship Jesus."

Leader • Was Aiden worshiping the way he should have been? What could he have done differently? Prayer is one way we worship, and it's a special time where we get to talk to God.

The wise men were not Jews. They probably didn't know everything about the one true God, but even they knew Jesus was a special child. They chose to really worship Him. *Why did the wise men visit Jesus? The wise men came to worship Jesus as King.*

Many times, the Old Testament talks about a future King whose rule will be forever. It's all about Jesus. He still deserves our worship today, and we should trust in Him and submit to Him as the King of our lives.

The Gospel: God's Plan for Me (optional)

Use Scripture and the guide provided with this session to explain to boys and girls how to become a Christian. Assign individuals to meet with kids who have more questions. If this is not possible, encourage boys and girls to ask their parents, small group leaders, and other Christian adults any questions they may have about becoming a Christian.

Prayer (3 minutes)

Show the big picture question slide or poster.

Leader • Before we move on, did anyone hear the answer to our big picture question? *Why did the wise men visit Jesus? The wise men came to worship Jesus as King.*

Group the kids by gender to be either kings or queens. Ask the boys (kings) to read the big picture question. Encourage the girls (queens) to read the answer. Allow the queens to ask the question and the kings to answer. Repeat as time allows.

Before transitioning to small group, make any necessary announcements. Lead the kids in prayer. Pray that kids will understand that Jesus came as our King to rule forever. Thank God that we can worship Jesus as King, too.

Dismiss to small groups

The Gospel: God's Plan for Me

Ask kids if they have ever heard the word *gospel*. Clarify that the word *gospel* means "good news." It is the message about Christ, the kingdom of God, and salvation. Use the following guide to share the gospel with kids.

God rules. Explain to kids that the Bible tells us God created everything, and He is in charge of everything. Invite a volunteer to read Genesis 1:1 from the Bible. Read Revelation 4:11 or Colossians 1:16-17 aloud and explain what these verses mean.

We sinned. Tell kids that since the time of Adam and Eve, everyone has chosen to disobey God (Romans 3:23). The Bible calls this sin. Because God is holy, God cannot be around sin. Sin separates us from God and deserves God's punishment of death (Romans 6:23).

God provided. Choose a child to read John 3:16 aloud. Say that God sent His Son Jesus, the perfect solution to our sin problem, to rescue us from the punishment we deserve. It's something we, as sinners, could never earn on our own. Jesus alone saves us. Read and explain Ephesians 2:8-9.

Jesus gives. Share with kids that Jesus lived a perfect life, died on the cross for our sins, and rose again. Because Jesus gave up His life for us, we can be welcomed into God's family for eternity. This is the best gift ever! Read Romans 5:8; 2 Corinthians 5:21; or 1 Peter 3:18.

We respond. Tell kids that they can respond to Jesus. Read Romans 10:9-10,13. Review these aspects of our response: Believe in your heart that Jesus alone saves you through what He's already done on the cross. Repent, turning from self and sin to Jesus. Tell God and others that your faith is in Jesus.

Offer to talk with any child who is interested in responding to Jesus.

Small Group LEADER

Session Title: Wise Men Visited Jesus
Bible Passage: Matthew 2:1-21
Big Picture Question: Why did the wise men visit Jesus? The wise men came to worship Jesus as King.
Key Passage: Luke 2:10-11
Unit Christ Connection: The Savior God had promised was born!

• Key Passage Slide or Poster (enhanced CD)
• marker
• dry erase board and markers (optional)
• gift tags or stickers, 1 per kid

Key passage activity (5 minutes)

Make sure the key passage, Luke 2:10-11, is visible for each child, either as the printed poster or written on a dry erase board. Read the verses together.

Say • The message to the shepherds was that a Savior was born—not just for them, but for all people then and now. The wise men remind us that Jesus is also King. He rules all of creation and desires us to obey Him as ruler of our lives as well. He wants us to trust Him with control of everything we do and say.

Before class, write the key passage on individual gift tags or stickers by writing three to four words on each one. Make two sets. Distribute a gift tag to each kid. Remind the kids that the best gift they can give to God is their lives—in trust and obedience. The kids are the "gifts" and must put themselves in the right order. If you have kids without a tag, let them help the other kids get in order. If you have too many tags, organize the passage in sections.

• Bibles, 1 per kid
• Small Group Visual Pack
• Big Picture Question Slide or Poster (enhanced CD)

Bible story review (10 minutes)

Encourage the kids to find Matthew 2 in their Bibles. Help them as needed.

Say • In which two books of the New Testament can we find the Christmas story? (*Matthew, Luke*) These books are two of four books called what? (*the Gospels*) Whose life do the Gospels tell us about? (*Jesus*) In which book do we find the story of the wise men? (*Matthew*)

Use the small group visual pack to show kids where today's Bible story is on the timeline. Review the Bible story provided or summarize the story in your own words.

Inform the kids that you want to play a game of fact or fiction about the wise men. Explain that some things we think are true about the wise men may not be true. You will read a statement. Encourage the kids who think the statement is a fact to run to the wall on the right side of the room. Those who think it is fiction should run to the wall on the left side of the room. Identify which wall is to the right and which is to the left. The statements are below:

1. The Bible says three wise men visited Jesus. (*Fiction. We assume there were three because of the three gifts, but the Bible doesn't say how many there were.*)

2. The wise men traveled from the east. (*Fact. They most likely traveled many, many miles to find Jesus.*)

3. The wise men were kings. (*Fiction. The wise men were* magi, *which means they used the stars to tell the future.*)

4. The wise men came on the night of Jesus' birth. (*Fiction. We don't know for sure when the wise men came. We know Herod had all boys under two years old killed, so Jesus was probably less than two. We also know they came to a home, not to the manger.*)

5. The wise men worshiped Jesus as King. (*Fact. They might not have understood how Jesus would be King, but they believed it to be true.*)

Say • The wise men are a reminder that Jesus did not just come as Savior; He also came as King. We should follow Him because we love and know Him.

Show the big picture question slide or poster.

Say • That brings us back to our big picture question. ***Why did the wise men visit Jesus? The wise men came to worship Jesus as King.***

Activity choice (10 minutes)

Option 1: Which gift?

Take three pieces of paper and write *gold* on one, *frankincense* on the second, and *myrrh* on the third. Fold each piece of paper and place in an empty gift bag. Choose a volunteer. Invite the volunteer to guess which bag has the gold. If she chooses correctly, allow her to shuffle the papers and again place each one in a bag. Continue inviting kids to try and find each gift for as long as time allows.

• paper, 3 pieces
• marker
• 3 gift bags or paper sacks

Say • Gold, frankincense, and myrrh were gifts perfect for a king. ***Why did the wise men visit Jesus? The wise men came to worship Jesus as King.***

Option 2: Mission bag

Distribute a bag to each child. Provide crayons or markers, and encourage the kids to color the bag to give to someone as a gift. Distribute other decorations if available. Once completed, invite the kids to fill the bag with a gift and give it away. (Gift ideas: cookies to take to a neighbor, toys that can go to a shelter, supplies that can go to a nursing home, and so forth.)

• white paper sacks or gift bags, 1 per child
• crayons or markers
• stickers (optional)

Say • The wise men were eager to give gifts to Jesus because they recognized Him as King. *Why did the wise men visit Jesus? The wise men came to worship Jesus as King.*

Journal and prayer (5 minutes)

- folder, 1 per kid
- Journal Page, 1 per kid (enhanced CD)
- markers or crayons
- Bible Story Coloring Page

Distribute each child's journal and the journal page provided with this session. Instruct the kids to draw the wise men visiting Jesus. Encourage kids who can write to put the key passage below the picture.

Say • Don't forget that you can worship Jesus as King, too. *Why did the wise men visit Jesus? The wise men came to worship Jesus as King.*

Make sure each child puts this week's sheet in his journal and then collect them. Keep the journals in the classroom so they will be available every week or as often as you wish to use them.

If time remains, take prayer requests or allow kids to color the coloring page provided with this session. End the session with prayer, thanking God for sending Jesus to rule forever. Pray for each child by name, and ask God to help each child submit to Jesus as King in his or her life.

Unit 5: GOD FORMED HIS NATION

Big Picture Questions

Session 1: Why did God save Moses? God saved Moses to rescue His people from captivity.

Session 2: What did God show the Egyptians and the Israelites? God showed that He is the one true God.

Session 3: Why is the Passover important? The Passover was the way God chose to save His people and is a picture of Christ's sacrifice for sinners.

Session 4: Is anything too hard for God to do? Nothing is impossible for God.

Unit 5: GOD FORMED HIS NATION

Unit Description: Joseph brought Jacob's family, 70 persons in all, to live in the land of Goshen. As the family grew into God's nation, over time they were enslaved by the Egyptian taskmasters. God sent Moses to rescue His people from oppression. Through mighty miracles, God saved His people and brought glory to His name.

Unit Key Passage: Exodus 6:7

Unit Christ Connection: God saved His people from physical captivity in Egypt as He would one day send Jesus to save His people from spiritual captivity.

Session 1: Moses Was Born and Called
Exodus 1:8–2:10,23-25; 3:1–4:20

Session 2: Moses Confronted Pharaoh
Exodus 5:1–6:13; 6:28–11:1

Session 3: The Passover
Exodus 11:1–13:16

Session 4: The Israelites Crossed the Red Sea
Exodus 13:17–17:7

Teacher BIBLE STUDY

Moses was born into a rough world. The Israelites were so great in number that the king of Egypt forced them into hard labor. The Israelites were ordered to make bricks to build houses and cities. When that didn't work, Pharaoh instituted an unimaginable method of population control: kill all of the baby boys. Pharaoh was afraid the boys would become men who would rise up against him.

Moses' story is a clear picture of God's sovereignty. Not only was Moses' life spared by the Egyptian princess, but also his mother nursed him and he grew up in the house of Pharaoh. God also planned for Moses to spend years shepherding in Midian before He called him to his task.

Imagine the encounter between God and Moses at the burning bush. God drew a curious Moses to Himself, and then He spoke to him: "Moses, Moses!"

God identified Himself as the God of Abraham, of Isaac, and of Jacob. He testified to His own grace: "I have observed the misery of My people … and I know about their sufferings.… I am sending you … so that you may lead My people, the Israelites, out of Egypt" (Ex. 3:7-10).

Perhaps God's greatest revelation to Moses was His name: "I AM WHO I AM." The most basic and important fact about God is that He exists—He always has and always will exist. He does not change. God revealed to Moses who He is so that Moses would trust in Him.

Help the kids you teach understand that God saved Moses for a special purpose: to rescue His people. Emphasize that the calling of Moses points to a greater calling and rescue—the call of Jesus to come to earth to save God's people from their sin. When kids better understand who God is, they can trust in Him.

Younger Kids BIBLE STUDY OVERVIEW

Session Title: Moses Was Born and Called
Bible Passage: Exodus 1:8–2:10,23-25; 3:1–4:20
Big Picture Question: Why did God save Moses? God saved Moses to rescue His people from captivity.
Key Passage: Exodus 6:7
Unit Christ Connection: God saved His people from physical captivity in Egypt as He would one day send Jesus to save His people from spiritual captivity.

Small Group Opening

Large Group Leader

Small Group Leader

God Formed His Nation

The BIBLE STORY

Moses Was Born and Called
Exodus 1:8–2:10,23-25; 3:1–4:20

Years after Joseph brought his family to Egypt to save them from famine, Joseph died. His family stayed in Egypt, and the family grew. The family was known as Israelites because they came from the family of Israel (Jacob). A new pharaoh came to power. He did not know about the wonderful things Joseph had done for Egypt.

The new king was afraid of the Israelites (also called Hebrews). There were so many of them! They might join their enemies and fight against Egypt! So the king made them slaves with very hard work to do. But the harder they worked, the bigger their families grew. The Egyptian king was desperate.

"Kill all the baby boys!" Pharaoh told the Hebrew midwives, who helped with births. "Let the girls live, but kill the boys!" But the midwives feared God more than they feared Pharaoh. They let the boys live. Pharaoh became angrier. "Throw every Hebrew baby boy into the Nile River!" he commanded.

Then a special baby was born. His mother hid him until she could no longer hide him. She put her baby boy in a basket and set it along the banks of the Nile. His older sister, Miriam, stayed nearby and watched the basket.

Soon Pharaoh's daughter, the princess, went to the river to bathe. She found the baby in the basket and felt sorry for him. Miriam offered to find a woman to nurse the baby until he was older. "Go!" said Pharaoh's daughter. Miriam brought her mother. The princess paid Moses' mother to care for him. The princess named the baby *Moses* because she drew him out of the water.

Moses never forgot that he was born a Hebrew. He saw how his people were poor and were forced to work very hard. One day Moses saw an Egyptian beating a Hebrew. Moses killed the Egyptian. Pharaoh found out and was angry.

Moses ran away to a place called Midian (MID ih uhn), where he became a shepherd for many years. The Israelite people in Egypt were still miserable, and they cried out to God. God heard their groaning. He planned to use Moses to answer their prayers.

One day after the pharaoh had died, while Moses was with the flock in the wilderness, he saw a burning bush. The Angel of the LORD was in the fire, and the bush was not burning up. How strange! Moses was curious and he went to look. Suddenly, God called from the bush, "Moses, Moses!"

Moses replied, "Here I am." God said, "Take off your sandals. This is holy ground. I have seen how My people are suffering. I want you to lead them out of Egypt to a good land I have for them. First, lead them into the wilderness so they can worship Me."

Moses doubted. He wondered if the Israelites even remembered God. "What if they ask for Your name?" Moses asked. "What should I tell them?"

"I AM WHO I AM," God said. "Tell them: I AM has sent me to you." God was saying that He exists, that He never changes, and that He lives forever.

God warned that leading the people out of Egypt would not be easy. Pharaoh would not let them go. But after miracles that God would perform, Pharaoh would let them go.

Moses was still stubborn. "What if they don't believe me and will not leave with me?" he asked. God gave Moses three miracles to perform to prove that God was with him. First, God turned Moses' staff into a snake. Then He made Moses' hand turn white with leprosy. Finally, God told Moses that if he poured water from the Nile onto the ground, it would turn into blood.

"Lord," Moses said, "I am not good at speaking. Please, send someone else." God was angry with Moses for asking God to send someone else, but He agreed to send Moses' brother, Aaron, with him.

The Israelites were suffering. They cried out to God and He heard their prayers. God was sending Moses to save them.

Christ Connection: God saved Moses for a special purpose: to rescue His people. The calling of Moses points to a greater calling and rescue— the call of Jesus to come to earth to save God's people from their sin. Moses and Jesus both obeyed God's commands in order to carry out His plan of salvation. Moses delivered God's people from physical captivity; Jesus delivered God's people from captivity to sin.

God Formed His Nation

Small Group OPENING

Session Title: Moses Was Born and Called
Bible Passage: Exodus 1:8–2:10,23-25; 3:1–4:20
Big Picture Question: Why did God save Moses? God saved Moses to rescue His people from captivity.
Key Passage: Exodus 6:7
Unit Christ Connection: God saved His people from physical captivity in Egypt as He would one day send Jesus to save His people from spiritual captivity.

Welcome time

Arriving Activity: Superhero powers

Engage kids in conversation as they enter the room. Ask the kids what powers they would want if they could be superheroes. Encourage them to act out their superhero powers for you.

Say • Superhero powers are not real, but God can use us for heroic things. Today, we will talk about a man God made into a hero.

Activity page (5 minutes)

• "Purpose Finder" activity page, 1 per kid
• pencils

Guide boys and girls to complete the activity page.

Say • Everyone has a purpose. God knows His plan for you already, and His plan may be very different than the one you have. Today, we will learn about someone who didn't understand what God was going to do in his life.

Session starter (10 minutes)

Option 1: I have

Invite the kids to sit in a large circle. Choose one volunteer to stand in the middle of the circle. That volunteer will say, "Have you ever …?" Instruct the volunteer to follow that phrase with something special she has done. The other kids who have done that will stand and quickly swap seats with others standing. The volunteer will try to get a seat, too. Whoever is left standing is the next volunteer. If kids struggle to come up with something, use the following possibilities to get started:

- Have you ever been to a theme park?
- Have you ever played in the rain?
- Have you ever been on a cruise ship?
- Have you ever ridden a train?
- Have you ever played a sport?

Say • Sometimes God will ask us to do something we have never done before. That's what happened to the man in today's story.

Option 2: Shoe game

Encourage the kids to take off their shoes and use them to form a large pile in the center of the room. Instruct the kids to form a large circle around the shoes. Mix up the shoes. Direct the kids to race to the pile, find their shoes, put them on, and get back to where they started as quick as possible. Repeat as time allows.

Say • In today's story, God told someone to remove his shoes because he was standing on holy ground.

Transition to large group

Large Group LEADER

Session Title: Moses Was Born and Called
Bible Passage: Exodus 1:8–2:10,23-25; 3:1–4:20
Big Picture Question: Why did God save Moses? God saved Moses to rescue His people from captivity.
Key Passage: Exodus 6:7
Unit Christ Connection: God saved His people from physical captivity in Egypt as He would one day send Jesus to save His people from spiritual captivity.

• room decorations

Suggested Theme Decoration Ideas: Use cloth or large sheets of tan or brown paper to create a desert background. Use blue cloth or paper to make a water fall streaming down the background and onto the front of the room. Place artificial or live plants around the river. Cover the rest of the front area with outdoor green carpet. Use one area of open space for an archaeological dig site. Use a small kids swimming pool as a sandbox and put brown paper around it. Place shovels, buckets, and other digging tools nearby.

Countdown

• countdown video

Show the countdown video as your kids arrive, and set it to end as large group time begins.

Introduce the session (1 minute)

• small shovel

[Large group leader enters carrying a small shovel.]
Leader • Have you ever dug up something before? Maybe you've dug into your sandbox or your parent's flower garden. We dig to plant things, to build things, and sometimes to find things. It's just fun to dig. Did you know some people dig for information about people who lived long ago? Some dig for old bones. Others dig for

---

Younger Kids Bible Study Leader Guide
Unit 5 • Session 1

lost cities. These people are called archaeologists. Can you say that word? The places where they dig are called archaeological sites or dig sites.

• Timeline Map

Timeline map (1 minute)

Leader • Speaking of archaeological sites, we have a story to dig up. Let's see if we can find our Bible site on the timeline map. We are starting a whole new unit. Wow, it's a bush on fire, but it doesn't look burned. Today's story is called "Moses Was Born and Called."

Big picture question (1 minute)

Leader • Have you ever thought about all the treasure you can find by looking into your Bible? The Bible has hundreds of stories that tell us one big story: God's plan to save us.

Guess what? You can't find all those treasures without your Bible, so let's see if you have yours. Hold it up if you have it. Great! Let's take a look at our big picture question. In a moment, we are going to dig in our Bible and find the answer. Our question is: ***Why did God save Moses?***

• "You Lift Me Up" song

Sing (5 minutes)

Leader • Many of the stories in your Bible are about people who had some really bad days. Have you ever had a bad day? God doesn't promise that we won't have bad days. He does promise that if we trust Him, He will lift us up or take care of us. That reminds me of a song. It's actually our theme song for the next few weeks. Let's listen and see if we can sing along, too.
Sing together "You Lift Me Up."

Key passage (4 minutes)

Leader • God is God on good days and bad days. We've already seen God lift up Noah, Abraham, Isaac, Jacob, and Joseph. If you remember, Joseph led his family to Egypt to save them, but things got rough there. God didn't forget them though. He sent a clear message, and that message is our key passage for the next four weeks.

Show the slide or poster of this unit's key passage, Exodus 6:7. Lead the boys and girls to read the verse together.

Leader • Yahweh is a special name for God, which we sometimes see in our Bible as LORD. God promised that He hadn't forgotten His people. Instead, He made it clear that He is the only God. The name *Yahweh* was so special to God's people that they would not say it aloud. We can sing it out though as our key passage song.

Sing together "I Am Yahweh!"

Tell the Bible story (10 minutes)

• "Moses Was Born and Called" video
• Bibles, 1 per kid
• Bible Story Picture Slide or Poster (enhanced CD)

Leader • I think we've had enough hints about our Bible story. Why don't we dig into God's Word and see more about our mighty God? As we look, remember our big picture question. *Why did God save Moses?* See if you can find the answer.

Open your Bible to Exodus 1. Choose to tell the Bible story in your own words using the script provided, or show the "Moses Was Born and Called" video.

Leader • Moses really had some good days and some bad days. He went from a baby the Egyptians wanted to kill to living like a prince. When he grew up and tried to stand up for his people, he had to leave the palace and become a shepherd. God had plans for Moses though. God had something great in mind for Moses since He saved Moses as a baby. ***Why did God save Moses? God saved Moses to rescue His people from captivity.*** *Captivity* means they were not free to do what they wanted or go where they wanted. God told Moses to tell everyone that I AM was sending him to rescue the Israelites. The name *I AM* tells us God is real and He never ever changes.

Ask the following review questions:

1. Where did Moses' mom put him when she couldn't hide him anymore? (*in a basket along the reeds of the Nile river, Exodus 2:3*)
2. Who found baby Moses? (*Pharaoh's daughter, Exodus 2:5-6*)
3. Why did Moses leave Egypt? (*Pharaoh was angry, Exodus 2:15*)
4. How did God appear to Moses? (*in a bush on fire that didn't burn up, Exodus 3:2*)
5. What did God tell Moses? (*go to Pharaoh and rescue God's people, Exodus 3:10*)

Discussion starter video (4 minutes)

• "Rope Climb" video

Leader • Have you ever faced something that seemed really hard? Maybe something like this has happened to you.

Play "Rope Climb."

Leader • Have you ever questioned whether or not you could do something? Have you ever failed at something? Moses must have felt like he had failed after running from Pharaoh's palace, leaving behind all his family and friends. Perhaps that's why he questioned God's choosing him to save the people. Moses' past didn't change God's plans to use Moses. ***Why did God save Moses? God saved Moses to rescue His people from captivity.*** God was about to make Moses a hero. That reminds me of a

far better hero. His name is Jesus. Moses was called to save God's people from being slaves to Egypt. We can't escape sin; we are slaves to sin. Jesus came to free us and save the world from sin.

The Gospel: God's Plan for Me (optional)

Use Scripture and the guide provided with this session to explain to boys and girls how to become a Christian. Assign individuals to meet with kids who have more questions. If this is not possible, encourage boys and girls to ask their parents, small group leaders, and other Christian adults any questions they may have about becoming a Christian.

Prayer (4 minutes)

Show the big picture question slide or poster.

Leader • Did you notice the big picture question and answer in our story today? *Why did God save Moses? God saved Moses to rescue His people from captivity.*

Ask the kids to spend a few minutes going around the room asking their friends the big picture question. Encourage those who are asked to give the answer.

Before transitioning to small group, make any necessary announcements. Lead the kids in prayer. Thank God for rescuing us from sin, and pray that kids will understand that God can use them no matter what they have done in the past.

Dismiss to small groups

• Big Picture Question
Slide or Poster
(enhanced CD

The Gospel: God's Plan for Me

Ask kids if they have ever heard the word *gospel*. Clarify that the word *gospel* means "good news." It is the message about Christ, the kingdom of God, and salvation. Use the following guide to share the gospel with kids.

God rules. Explain to kids that the Bible tells us God created everything, and He is in charge of everything. Invite a volunteer to read Genesis 1:1 from the Bible. Read Revelation 4:11 or Colossians 1:16-17 aloud and explain what these verses mean.

We sinned. Tell kids that since the time of Adam and Eve, everyone has chosen to disobey God (Romans 3:23). The Bible calls this sin. Because God is holy, God cannot be around sin. Sin separates us from God and deserves God's punishment of death (Romans 6:23).

God provided. Choose a child to read John 3:16 aloud. Say that God sent His Son Jesus, the perfect solution to our sin problem, to rescue us from the punishment we deserve. It's something we, as sinners, could never earn on our own. Jesus alone saves us. Read and explain Ephesians 2:8-9.

Jesus gives. Share with kids that Jesus lived a perfect life, died on the cross for our sins, and rose again. Because Jesus gave up His life for us, we can be welcomed into God's family for eternity. This is the best gift ever! Read Romans 5:8; 2 Corinthians 5:21; or 1 Peter 3:18.

We respond. Tell kids that they can respond to Jesus. Read Romans 10:9-10,13. Review these aspects of our response: Believe in your heart that Jesus alone saves you through what He's already done on the cross. Repent, turning from self and sin to Jesus. Tell God and others that your faith is in Jesus.

Offer to talk with any child who is interested in responding to Jesus.

Small Group LEADER

Session Title: Moses Was Born and Called
Bible Passage: Exodus 1:8–2:10,23-25; 3:1–4:20
Big Picture Question: Why did God save Moses? God saved Moses to rescue His people from captivity.
Key Passage: Exodus 6:7
Unit Christ Connection: God saved His people from physical captivity in Egypt as He would one day send Jesus to save His people from spiritual captivity.

Key passage activity (5 minutes)

- Key Passage Slide or Poster (enhanced CD)
- dry erase board and markers (optional)

Make sure the key passage, Exodus 6:7, is visible for each child, either as the printed poster or written on a dry erase board. Read the verse together.

Say • Moses was commanded to tell God's people who the LORD was. God had not forgotten His original covenant to Abraham to bless his family. God had heard the cries of His people and was preparing to free them, using Moses. *Why did God save Moses? God saved Moses to rescue His people from captivity.*

Repeat the key passage as a group several times. Give each child a number, starting at one. Invite "one" to read the first word, "two" to read the second word, and so forth. If you have more kids than words, start back at one.

Bible story review (10 minutes)

- Bibles, 1 per kid
- Small Group Visual Pack
- Big Picture Question Slide or Poster (enhanced CD)

Encourage the kids to find Exodus 1 in their Bibles. Help them as needed.

Say • Is Exodus found in the Old Testament or New Testament? (*Old Testament*) Where in the Old Testament is Exodus? (*second book*) What division of the Bible is Exodus in? (*Law*) Exodus tell us how God used Moses to rescue His people from Egypt. Use the small group visual pack to show kids where today's Bible story is on the timeline. Review the Bible story provided or summarize the story in your own words. Read the statements below. Instruct the kids to decide if this happened to Moses as a child or as an adult. Encourage kids who believe it happened when Moses was a child to crouch down. If they believe it happened when he was an adult, they should stand on their toes.

- Moses was hidden in a basket. (*child*)
- God spoke to Moses in a burning bush. (*adult*)
- Miriam helped Moses. (*child*)
- Moses lived in Pharaoh's house. (*child*)
- Moses was a shepherd. (*adult*)
- Moses rescued God's people from captivity. (*adult*)

Say • Moses' experiences as a prince in Pharaoh's palace and as a shepherd in Midian were both part of God's plan for him.

Show the big picture question slide or poster.

Say • Let's take one last look at our big picture question and answer. ***Why did God save Moses? God saved Moses to rescue His people from captivity.*** We have someone who rescues us from captivity, too. Because of sin, we are held captive by Satan, the Evil One. Jesus came to rescue us from Satan and from our sin. Because of Jesus, we are free again.

Use Scripture and the following guide to explain to boys and girls how to become a Christian.

- **God rules.** God created and is in charge of everything. (Gen. 1:1; Rev. 4:11; Col. 1:16-17)
- **We sinned.** Since Adam and Eve, everyone has chosen to disobey God. (Rom. 3:23; 6:23)

- **God provided.** God sent His Son Jesus to rescue us from the punishment we deserve. (John 3:16; Eph. 2:8-9)
- **Jesus gives.** Jesus lived a perfect life, died on the cross for our sins, and rose again so we can be welcomed into God's family. (Rom. 5:8; 2 Cor. 5:21; 1 Pet. 3:18)
- **We respond.** Believe that Jesus alone saves you. Repent. Tell God that your faith is in Jesus. (Rom. 10:9-10,13)

Activity choice (10 minutes)

Option 1: Finding Moses

Choose a volunteer to play the part of a detective. Instruct the rest of the kids to stand shoulder to shoulder in a line or circle. Invite the detective to look closely because in a moment someone will be missing. Tell the detective that the person missing will be "Moses." The detective must stand in the corner facing the wall. Quietly choose someone to play Moses. Tell the kids to swap places and hide Moses behind them. The detective must guess who is Moses. Repeat with a new detective and Moses.

Say • Moses was hidden from Pharaoh as a child and then ran from Pharaoh as an adult, but God had big plans for him. *Why did God save Moses? God saved Moses to rescue His people from captivity.*

Option 2: Burning bush

- construction paper or heavyweight paper
- orange, red, and yellow tissue paper
- black or brown marker, 1 per kid

Distribute a piece of white construction paper or heavyweight paper. Encourage kids to use a black or brown marker to trace one hand with fingers spread apart on the paper. Instruct them to shade in the handprint. Provide small squares of orange, red, and yellow tissue paper to each child. Demonstrate how to put a small dot of glue in the center of a piece of the tissue paper. Outline the handprint, which is the bush, with the tissue paper squares, which is the fire. Show the kids how to fluff the edges of each square to give the picture a 3-D look.

Say • God spoke to Moses through a bush that was on fire but didn't burn. God saved Moses as a child, so he would rescue God's people. *Why did God save Moses? God saved Moses to rescue His people from captivity.*

Journal and prayer (5 minutes)

- folder, 1 per kid
- Journal Page, 1 per kid (enhanced CD)
- markers or crayons
- Bible Story Coloring Page

Distribute each child's journal and the journal page provided with this session. Instruct the kids to draw Moses in a basket on one side and a burning bush on the other. Older kids can write a paragraph of this story in their own words below their picture.

Say • Don't forget the big picture question and answer for today? *Why did God save Moses? God saved Moses to rescue His people from captivity.*

Make sure each child puts this week's sheet in his journal and then collect them. Keep the journals in the classroom so they will be available every week or as often as you wish to use them.

If time remains, take prayer requests or allow kids to color the coloring page provided with this session. End the session with prayer, thanking God for rescuing us from our sins. Pray for each child by name, and ask God to help each kid tell others about Jesus' rescue.

Teacher BIBLE STUDY

Moses' appeals to Pharaoh to let the Israelites go were not well received. Time and time again, God hardened Pharaoh's heart, and Pharaoh refused to let the people go. Wait a second. God hardened Pharaoh's heart? Wasn't God the One wanting the Israelites out of Egypt? Why would he do such a thing?

God did not contradict Himself. He has a special purpose behind everything He does. Moses confronted Pharaoh and said, "This is what Yahweh, the God of Israel, says: Let My people go, so that they may hold a festival for Me in the wilderness." Note Pharaoh's response: "Who is Yahweh that I should obey Him by letting Israel go?" (Ex. 5:1-2)

Pharaoh did not recognize God's authority. The Egyptians worshiped false gods like Ra, the sun god, and Hapi, the god of the Nile. God explained His plan to Moses and Aaron: "I will harden Pharaoh's heart and multiply My signs and wonders in the land of Egypt. Pharaoh will not listen to you, but I will put My hand on Egypt and bring the divisions of My people the Israelites out of the land of Egypt by great acts of judgment. The Egyptians will know that I am Yahweh when I stretch out My hand against Egypt, and bring out the Israelites from among them" (Ex. 7:3-5).

The plagues were acts of judgment designed to show the Egyptians who God is. And they learned their lesson. Read Exodus 8:19; 9:20,27; and 10:7.

As you teach children about God's mighty works and Moses' obedience to God, invite them to think about Jesus. God called Moses to be His servant. He was a great servant who obeyed God and led the Israelites out of slavery. The Bible says that Jesus is greater than Moses. (Heb. 3:3) Jesus was a servant who obeyed God perfectly and suffered to free His people from sin.

Younger Kids BIBLE STUDY OVERVIEW

Session Title: Moses Confronted Pharaoh
Bible Passage: Exodus 5:1–6:13; 6:28–11:1
Big Picture Question: What did God show the Egyptians and the Israelites? God showed that He is the one true God.
Key Passage: Exodus 6:7
Unit Christ Connection: God saved His people from physical captivity in Egypt as He would one day send Jesus to save His people from spiritual captivity.

Small Group Opening

Large Group Leader

Small Group Leader

The BIBLE STORY

Moses Confronted Pharaoh
Exodus 5:1–6:13; 6:28–11:1

After God called Moses to save His people from Egypt, Moses and Aaron went to talk to Pharaoh. "This is what Yahweh the God of Israel says," they said. "Let My people go, so that they may worship Me in the wilderness."

But Pharaoh responded, "Who is this Yahweh? Why should I obey Him? I do not know Him! Israel may not go!" Pharaoh was angry because he thought Moses was just trying to stop the people from working hard. He made work even harder for the people of Israel. "You are slackers!" he told them. "That is why you want to go to worship your God."

The Israelites were not happy with Moses. "You are making trouble for us," they said. Moses went back to God and asked, "Why did you send me? You haven't saved your people at all!"

God again promised that the Israelites would be free. "Pharaoh will not listen to you, but you must do exactly what I say. I am going to show Pharaoh who I am," God said. God promised to fight for His people.

Moses and Aaron returned to Pharaoh. They performed a miracle to show that God was with them. Moses' staff turned into a snake. Pharaoh still would not listen to them.

God knew that Pharaoh would not let the Israelites go. God explained, "Pharaoh's heart is hard: he refuses to let the people go." So God sent a set of plagues, or punishments, to the Egyptians. He judged their sin.

First, God turned the water in the Nile River into blood. The fish in the Nile died, and the river smelled so bad that the Egyptians could not drink from it. There was blood everywhere! But Pharaoh turned and went into his palace. He would not let the people go.

Second, God sent frogs into Egypt. Aaron stretched his hand over the waters of Egypt, and frogs came up and covered the land. "Ask your God to take the frogs away," Pharaoh said. "Then I will let the people go." The next day, God removed the frogs. When Pharaoh saw that they were gone, he refused to let the people go.

Third, God sent gnats into Egypt. Gnats are small flies that bite people and animals. Pharaoh's magicians said, "God did this," but Pharaoh's heart hardened, and he would not let the people go.

Fourth, God sent flies into Egypt. Flies were everywhere! But no flies swarmed where the Israelites lived. "Let My people go!" "I will let them go," Pharaoh said. Then he changed his mind. He did not let the people go.

Fifth, God caused all the livestock in the fields—the horses, donkeys, camels, and sheep—to die. All of the livestock in the fields of Egypt died, but none of the Israelites' animals died. Pharaoh's heart was hardened again. He did not let the people go.

Sixth, God sent boils, or sore spots, all over the people in Egypt. The people were covered with sores. Pharaoh's heart was hard. He did not listen to Moses, just like God had said.

Seventh, God sent a hailstorm to Egypt. It was the worst storm they had ever seen! Every plant was smashed and every tree was broken. "Let My people go!" "I will let you go," Pharaoh said. But as soon as the hail stopped, Pharaoh would not let the people go.

Eighth, God sent locusts, or grasshoppers, into Egypt. They ate every living plant. Moses said, "This is what God says: Let My people go!" "Go worship your God," Pharaoh said. But as soon as the locusts were gone, Pharaoh refused to let the Israelites go.

Next, God sent darkness to cover the land. For three days, no one could see anything, but the Israelites had light. Pharaoh was unwilling to let them go. "Get away from me!" Pharaoh told Moses.

God told Moses, "I will bring one more plague on Pharaoh and on Egypt. After that, Pharaoh will let you go."

Christ Connection: God called Moses to be His servant. He was a great servant who obeyed God and led the Israelites out of slavery. The Bible says that Jesus is greater than Moses. (Hebrews 3:3) Jesus was a servant who obeyed God perfectly and suffered to free His people from sin.

God Formed His Nation

Small Group OPENING

Session Title: Moses Confronted Pharaoh
Bible Passage: Exodus 5:1–6:13; 6:28–11:1
Big Picture Question: What did God show the Egyptians and the Israelites? God showed that He is the one true God.
Key Passage: Exodus 6:7
Unit Christ Connection: God saved His people from physical captivity in Egypt as He would one day send Jesus to save His people from spiritual captivity.

• tape or stickers

Welcome time

Arriving Activity: Jump, jump

Tape a start line. As kids arrive, encourage them to see who can jump the farthest. Mark their spots with tape or allow them to mark their spots with stickers.

Say • Jumping reminds me of a frog. That reminds me of today's Bible story, where a whole bunch of frogs suddenly appeared.

• "Oh, Gnats!" activity page, 1 per kid
• pencils

Activity page (5 minutes)

Guide boys and girls to complete the activity page.

Say • Imagine gnats everywhere, tiny little bugs landing all over you and everything else. Now imagine God using those gnats to teach two nations—and even us—something very important.

• paper wads, 5 or 6
• tape

Session starter (10 minutes)

Option 1: Hailstones

Tape a large circle on the floor that is big enough for all the kids to stand on. Invite the kids to stand on the tape around the circle. Choose a volunteer to stand outside the circle, facing away from the kids. Instruct the kids to walk around the circle until the volunteer says "hailstorm coming." The volunteer then counts slowly to three. The kids must find a place in the circle and freeze before the volunteer gets to three. The volunteer then tosses the paperwads over his shoulder. The volunteer may not look back at the kids at any point in the game. Any kid who gets hit by a hailstone or moves to keep from getting hit is out. Use one of the kids who is out to be the next volunteer. Repeat and then let all the kids who are out return to play again.

Say • God used a hailstorm as part of His plan to show the Egyptians that only He is God.

Option 2: Moses mix

Provide each child with a ziplock bag, a paper towel, and a tablespoon of any or all of the following options: raisins, small marshmallows, twisted pretzels, candy-coated chocolate pieces, and animal crackers. Explain that everyone is pretending the raisins are gnats; the small marshmallows are hailstones; the pretzels are locusts; the candy-coated chocolate pieces are boils; and the animal crackers are livestock or farm animals.

Say • The items in this snack remind us of some plagues God used to free His people in today's story.

Transition to large group

• ziplock bag, 1 per kid
• raisins
• small marshmallows
• twisted pretzels
• candy-coated chocolate pieces
• animal crackers

Tip: Consider food allergy issues when choosing snack items. Ask children or their parents for any allergy information, or post an allergy alert on the door where parents can see it.

Large Group LEADER

Session Title: Moses Confronted Pharaoh
Bible Passage: Exodus 5:1–6:13; 6:28–11:1
Big Picture Question: What did God show the Egyptians and the Israelites? God showed that He is the one true God.
Key Passage: Exodus 6:7
Unit Christ Connection: God saved His people from physical captivity in Egypt as He would one day send Jesus to save His people from spiritual captivity.

• countdown video

Countdown

Show the countdown video as your kids arrive, and set it to end as large group time begins.

• magnifying glass

Introduce the session (1 minute)

[Large group leader enters with a magnifying glass.]
Leader • Does anyone know what I have in my hand? That's right! It's a magnifying glass. What do you use a magnifying glass for? You use it to make something look bigger or to help you find something. An archaeologist might need one of these to look for very small things at a dig site. Remember, archaeologists dig for clues about people from long ago to see how they lived.

• Timeline Map

Timeline map (1 minute)

Leader • We don't need a magnifying glass to see where we are headed next on our timeline map. Last week, we got to see God tell Moses that he would free God's people from the Egyptians who had made the Israelites slaves. God promised to bring judgment on the Egyptians. This week, we have a bunch of frogs in this picture. Does anyone know of a Bible story with a bunch of frogs?

The title of today's Bible story is "Moses Confronted Pharaoh."

Big picture question (1 minute)

Leader • It's time for a Bible check. Get out your Bible, and let's see it. You don't have to dig or have a magnifying glass to learn about everything from creation to what will happen at the end of our lives. All of time is captured in this book. Every time you look into God's Word, you can discover more about God and His love for you through Jesus.

We will soon magnify our story for today. That means we have to see our big picture question. *What did God show the Egyptians and the Israelites?*

Sing (5 minutes)

• "You Lift Me Up" song

Leader • God had a message to deliver to the Egyptians, and He has a message for each of us. He wants us to understand that we have someone who took our punishment for sin. Moses was called to save God's people because they could not save themselves. We can't save ourselves from sin either, so Jesus came to take our punishment. Jesus died on the cross to make the way for all people to be saved. We are lifted up by His sacrifice. Sing together "You Lift Me Up."

Key passage (4 minutes)

• "I Am Yahweh!" song
• Key Passage Slide or Poster (enhanced CD)

Leader • Our key passage is from our story today. God sent Moses this message to give to His people, the Israelites.

Show the slide or poster of this unit's key passage, Exodus 6:7. Lead the boys and girls to read the verse together.

Leader • God sent the same message to the Egyptians and the Israelites, but He did it in two different ways. He rescued the Israelites as He promised Abraham, but He judged the Egyptians for their sin against Him. Let's see if we can remember our key passage by singing this song. Sing together "I Am Yahweh!"

Tell the Bible story (10 minutes)

• "Moses Confronted Pharaoh" video
• Bibles, 1 per kid
• Bible Story Picture Slide or Poster (enhanced CD)

Leader • Let's magnify or look closer at God's Word to see if we can spot the answer to our big picture question. *What did God show the Egyptians and the Israelites?* Open your Bible to Exodus 5. Choose to tell the Bible story in your own words using the script provided, or show the "Moses Confronted Pharaoh" video.

Leader • Pharaoh refused to let God's people go and worship God. Instead, Pharaoh treated them even worse after Moses' request. God was not surprised by Pharaoh's decision. He reminded Moses that Pharaoh would not let God's people go because God wanted to show Pharaoh that God was really God. The Egyptians worshiped gods who were not real. *What did God show the Egyptians and the Israelites? God showed that He is the one true God.* God punished Egypt with nine plagues. A *plague* is a disease or event that harms a lot of people. God used the plagues as mighty works that showed His power. They also showed that the gods the Egyptians worshiped did not have any power because they didn't even exist.

Ask the following review questions:

1. What did Pharaoh do when Moses first asked for him to let the Israelites go? (*He refused and gave the Israelites more work; Exodus 5:2,7-8*)

2. What did God say He was going to do to force Pharaoh to free His people? (*perform signs and*

wonders, great acts of judgement, or plagues; Exodus 7:3-4)

3. What did Aaron's staff turn into when thrown down before Pharaoh? (*a serpent or snake, Exodus 7:10*)

4. How many plagues did Egypt suffer through with Pharaoh still refusing to let the people go? (*9*)

5. Who does the Bible say is greater than Moses? (*Jesus, Hebrews 3:3*)

Discussion starter video (4 minutes)

• "One True God" video

Leader • Have you ever met someone who didn't go to church or believe in God? Watch this video.

Play "One True God."

Leader • What would you say if someone told you something like that? Is there more than one God? ***What did God show the Egyptians and the Israelites? God showed that He is the one true God.*** Maybe you don't worship another god, but you put school, sports, or video games before God. God wants to be first in your life. He loves you and wants others to see His glory through you. That's why He sent someone to save you from your sins. God used Moses to physically save the Israelites, but it is Jesus who spiritually saves us. He suffered and died on a cross so we wouldn't have to be punished for our sins.

The Gospel: God's Plan for Me (optional)

Use Scripture and the guide provided with this session to explain to boys and girls how to become a Christian. Assign individuals to meet with kids who have more questions. If this is not possible, encourage boys and girls to ask their parents, small group leaders, and other Christian adults any questions they may have about becoming a Christian.

God Formed His Nation

Prayer (4 minutes)

Show the big picture question slide or poster.

Leader • What an awesome big picture question! Did you find the answer? *What did God show the Egyptians and the Israelites? God showed that He is the one true God.* Ask the kids to each stand on one leg and try to say the big picture question and answer. Invite them to see how many times they can say it before having to put the other leg down.

Before transitioning to small group, make any necessary announcements. Lead the kids in prayer. Thank God for showing us who He is, and pray that kids will put God first as the one true God.

Dismiss to small groups

The Gospel: God's Plan for Me

Ask kids if they have ever heard the word *gospel*. Clarify that the word *gospel* means "good news." It is the message about Christ, the kingdom of God, and salvation. Use the following guide to share the gospel with kids.

God rules. Explain to kids that the Bible tells us God created everything, and He is in charge of everything. Invite a volunteer to read Genesis 1:1 from the Bible. Read Revelation 4:11 or Colossians 1:16-17 aloud and explain what these verses mean.

We sinned. Tell kids that since the time of Adam and Eve, everyone has chosen to disobey God (Romans 3:23). The Bible calls this sin. Because God is holy, God cannot be around sin. Sin separates us from God and deserves God's punishment of death (Romans 6:23).

God provided. Choose a child to read John 3:16 aloud. Say that God sent His Son Jesus, the perfect solution to our sin problem, to rescue us from the punishment we deserve. It's something we, as sinners, could never earn on our own. Jesus alone saves us. Read and explain Ephesians 2:8-9.

Jesus gives. Share with kids that Jesus lived a perfect life, died on the cross for our sins, and rose again. Because Jesus gave up His life for us, we can be welcomed into God's family for eternity. This is the best gift ever! Read Romans 5:8; 2 Corinthians 5:21; or 1 Peter 3:18.

We respond. Tell kids that they can respond to Jesus. Read Romans 10:9-10,13. Review these aspects of our response: Believe in your heart that Jesus alone saves you through what He's already done on the cross. Repent, turning from self and sin to Jesus. Tell God and others that your faith is in Jesus.

Offer to talk with any child who is interested in responding to Jesus.

Small Group LEADER

Session Title: Moses Confronted Pharaoh
Bible Passage: Exodus 5:1–6:13; 6:28–11:1
Big Picture Question: What did God show the Egyptians and the Israelites? God showed that He is the one true God.
Key Passage: Exodus 6:7
Unit Christ Connection: God saved His people from physical captivity in Egypt as He would one day send Jesus to save His people from spiritual captivity.

- Key Passage Slide or Poster (enhanced CD)
- dry erase board and markers (optional)

Key passage activity (5 minutes)

Make sure the key passage, Exodus 6:7, is visible for each child, either as the printed poster or written on a dry erase board. Read the verse together.

Say • The Israelites should not have been surprised to learn that God was going to save them. God promised Abraham, Isaac, and Jacob that He would bless their family. Their family grew into a large nation during the 400 years in Egypt, and they seemed to forget about God's promise. He sent them a reminder through the plagues. God's promised blessing is still true for those who know and love Him. Our blessing is that Jesus came to save us and take our punishment for sin.

Form two groups with the same number of kids. Instruct the two groups to line up single file in their groups and place the groups where the first kid in each line is face-to-face with the other. The kid in front of each line will say the first word of the key passage and hurry to the back of the line. The second kid will say the second word and move to the back of the line. Continue and see which group can finish the verse first. Repeat.

• Bibles, 1 per kid
• Small Group Visual Pack
• Big Picture Question Slide or Poster (enhanced CD)

Bible story review (10 minutes)

Encourage the kids to find Exodus 5 in their Bibles. Help them as needed.

Say • Which book is Exodus in the Old Testament? (*second book*) What division of the Bible is Exodus in? (*Law*) What story does Exodus tell us? (*how God used Moses to rescue His people from Egypt*)

Use the small group visual pack to show kids where today's Bible story is on the timeline. Review the Bible story provided or summarize the story in your own words. Talk about the plagues after you review the story. Read them in order, identifying which came first, second, third, and so forth. Once you have gone through them in order, read them out of order, and ask the kids to guess the number of the plague by holding up their fingers. They are listed in order below.

1. The waters of the Nile turned to blood. (*Ex. 7:14-25*)
2. Frogs filled the land of Egypt. (*Ex. 8:1-15*)
3. Gnats filled the land of Egypt. (*Ex. 8:16-19*)
4. Flies swarmed Egypt. (*Ex. 8:20-32*)
5. A disease killed the Egyptians cattle. (*Ex. 9:1-7*)
6. A skin disease caused boils to appear on the Egyptians' skin. (*Ex. 9:8-12*)
7. Hail killed everything not under a roof, including their plants. (*Ex. 9:13-35*)
8. Locusts destroyed any of the plants or trees the hail did not. (*Ex. 10:1-20*)
9. A deep darkness covered Egypt for three days. (*Ex. 10:21-29*)

Say • The plagues were events that only God could do. Show the big picture question slide or poster.

Say • That brings us to our big picture question and

answer. *What did God show the Egyptians and the Israelites? God showed that He is the one true God.*

Activity choice (10 minutes)

Option 1: Swarming plagues

Group kids into even teams of frogs, locusts, flies, and gnats. Divide the room in half with a piece of tape. Add another piece of tape across the room about five feet before the wall. The two pieces of tape should run the same direction. The area between this tape and the wall is the safe zone.

Invite all of the kids to swarm (constantly move) on the side of the room without the piece of tape near the wall. Frogs and locusts must jump while flies and gnats must move with hands out like wings. Flies and gnats cannot fly in a straight line. They must zigzag. The teacher or leader will call out "plague," followed by "frogs," "locusts," "flies," or "gnats." The kids in the group you called will try to tag the others before they cross into the safe zone. Those who make it across without getting tagged win. Repeat, calling out a different plague.

Say • God used nine different plagues to show something to the Egyptians and Israelites. *What did God show the Egyptians and the Israelites? God showed that He is the one true God.*

• tape

Option 2: One finger

Distribute half a foam sheet to each kid along with one template of the foam finger printable included with this session. Invite the kids to cut out the template and trace around it with a pencil or pen onto the piece of foam. Cut out the foam finger along the outline. Glue a magnet to the back of the finger.

• foam sheet, 1 per 2 kids
• "Foam Finger Template," 1 per kid (enhanced CD)
• pencil or pen
• glue
• magnet, 1 per kid
• scissors

Say • Foam fingers are common at sporting events to show that your team is number one. ***What did God show the Egyptians and the Israelites? God showed that He is the one true God.***

• folder, 1 per kid
• Journal Page, 1 per kid (enhanced CD)
• markers or crayons
• Bible Story Coloring Page

Journal and prayer (5 minutes)

Distribute each child's journal and the journal page provided with this session. Instruct the kids to draw a picture of at least one of the plagues. Older kids can write the plagues in the order they happened.

Say • Quick, someone tell me the answer to the big picture question. ***What did God show the Egyptians and the Israelites? God showed that He is the one true God.***

Make sure each child puts this week's sheet in her journal and then collect them. Keep the journals in the classroom so they will be available every week or as often as you wish to use them.

If time remains, take prayer requests or allow kids to color the coloring page provided with this session. End the session with prayer, thanking God for making it clear that He is our one true God. Pray for each child by name, and ask God to help each kid tell others that God is the one true God.

Teacher BIBLE STUDY

The tenth plague was the most severe and had the greatest impact on the Egyptian people. God told Moses that around midnight, every firstborn male in Egypt would die. No one would be excluded. Even the firstborn of the livestock would die.

But God gave specific instructions to the Israelites. They were to slaughter a lamb or goat and put its blood on their doorposts. The blood on the doorpost would be a distinguishing mark. When God saw the blood, He "passed over" the house.

The Israelite people were sinful, and they deserved death just as much as the Egyptians did. But God, by His grace, provided them a way out. By marking their doorposts with the blood of a lamb, they were spared from the judgment and death they deserved. They deserved to die; the lamb was killed instead.

The tenth plague happened just as the Lord said. The Lord struck every firstborn male in the land of Egypt. There wasn't a house without someone dead. Pharaoh had finally had enough. "Get up, leave my people, … and go, worship Yahweh as you have asked," he said. (See Exodus 12:29-31.)

As Christians, we are redeemed "with the precious blood of Christ, like that of a lamb without defect or blemish" (1 Peter 1:18-19). The heart of the gospel is found in the story of the Passover: Jesus was crucified, not for His sins, but for our sins. We deserve death, but He died instead.

Jesus is "the Lamb of God, who takes away the sin of the world" (John 1:29). His death was the ultimate sacrifice, and those who are under His saving blood will be passed over in the final judgment. God gave the Passover to show us His loving provision for sinful man to be made right with Him.

Younger Kids BIBLE STUDY OVERVIEW

Session Title: The Passover
Bible Passage: Exodus 11:1–13:16
Big Picture Question: Why is the Passover important? The Passover was the way God chose to save His people and is a picture of Christ's sacrifice for sinners.
Key Passage: Exodus 6:7
Unit Christ Connection: God saved His people from physical captivity in Egypt as He would one day send Jesus to save His people from spiritual captivity.

Small Group Opening

Large Group Leader

Small Group Leader

God Formed His Nation

The BIBLE STORY

The Passover
Exodus 11:1–13:16

No, no, no, no! Pharaoh refused over and over to let the Israelites go. "I will bring one more plague on Pharaoh and on Egypt," God said. "After that, he will let you go from here." Moses confronted Pharaoh and told him exactly what would happen: "About midnight God will go through Egypt, and every firstborn male in the land of Egypt will die, from Pharaoh's firstborn to the firstborn of the servant girl. Even the firstborn of the livestock will die. There will be a great cry in Egypt, but none of the Israelites will be harmed. Then you and your officials will come down and bow before me and tell us to leave."

Despite Moses' warning, Pharaoh did not let the Israelites go. So the tenth plague would happen as God had planned.

God gave to the Israelites specific instructions to prepare for that night. Every Israelite family would kill a lamb or goat and sprinkle its blood on the doorposts of their houses. This would be a special mark that God would see and "pass over" the houses of the Israelites. No one in their families would die.

God also told them to eat the lamb as a meal at midnight. The lamb was to be unblemished: no broken bones, no marks, no deformities. They were also to eat unleavened bread (bread without yeast) and bitter herbs. God said, "When you eat it, get dressed and put on your sandals. Eat the meal quickly and be ready to go!"

The Israelites' families obeyed God's instructions and got everything ready. While the Egyptians were sleeping, the Israelites were busy making a meal and putting blood on their doorposts.

Then, at midnight, God struck every firstborn in the land of Egypt. Pharaoh's son died. The prisoner's son died. The firstborn of the livestock died. There was a great cry in the land of Egypt because there wasn't a house without someone dead. Pharaoh called for Moses and Aaron and said, "Get up, leave my people, and go, worship Yahweh as you have asked."

The Israelites were ready! A whole army of them—600,000 men and their families—left Egypt quickly. They took with them bread and their animals. The Israelites even asked the Egyptians for their riches, and the Egyptians were so afraid that they handed them over!

God lead His people out of Egypt. He was preparing a place for them in a land called Canaan (KAY nuhn). For 430 years, the Israelites had been slaves in the land of Egypt. They were finally free!

Christ Connection: By His grace, God spared the Israelites from judgment by requiring the blood of a lamb. Jesus is the Lamb of God, who takes away the sin of the world. His death was the ultimate sacrifice, and those who trust in Christ are under His saving blood and will be passed over in the final judgment.

Small Group OPENING

Session Title: The Passover

Bible Passage: Exodus 11:1–13:16

Big Picture Question: Why is the Passover important? The Passover was the way God chose to save His people and is a picture of Christ's sacrifice for sinners.

Key Passage: Exodus 6:7

Unit Christ Connection: God saved His people from physical captivity in Egypt as He would one day send Jesus to save His people from spiritual captivity.

Welcome time

• Lord's Supper display (elements or picture, optional)

Arriving Activity: Lord's Supper

Take a few moments to talk about the Lord's Supper.

Display an example of the elements of the Lord's Supper.

Say • Have you ever heard of the Lord's Supper?
  • What does the cracker or bread represent?
  • What does the juice represent?

Activity page (5 minutes)

• "Journey Bound" activity page, 1 per kid
• pencils

Guide boys and girls to complete the activity page.

Say • God's special people, the Israelites, would begin a very long journey in today's story. We will see how they prepared and what they brought with them.

Session starter (10 minutes)

Option 1: Protected one

Choose two volunteers. Invite them to face away from the kids while you silently give two of the remaining

• strips of red paper, 2

kids a piece of red paper. Tell the two kids chosen that they must hide their piece of paper in a pocket or in their hand. Explain the game to the kids. The two volunteers are "snatchers." Designate a corner for each "snatcher" to bring his captured players to. Those with a small red piece of paper are "protected ones." The "protected ones" cannot be captured. If a "snatcher" chooses one of the "protected ones," the protected one must show the red paper. Once that happens, that "snatcher" may not capture anyone else. The other "snatcher"may continue until she captures a "protected one." The winner is the "snatcher" who captures the most kids. Choose new "snatchers" and "protected ones" and play again.

Say • How did it feel to be protected from the snatcher? We all like to be protected. In today's story, we will see how God's people were protected from one final plague on Pharaoh and Egypt.

Option 2: Door hanger

- foam sheet cut into 3-inch strips, 1 strip per kid
- 8- or 16-ounce cup, 1 per kid
- scissors, 1 per kid
- permanent markers
- stickers or other decorations (optional)

Before class, cut foam sheets widthwise into three-inch strips. Provide each child with one strip of foam. Provide an 8- or 16-ounce cup for every two or three kids. Invite the kids to trace a circle at the top of the foam lengthwise using the 8-ounce cup top or the 16-ounce cup bottom. Encourage them to center the circle from side to side and leave a small amount of foam at the top. Distribute scissors, permanent markers, stickers, and any other decorations you choose. Allow the kids to cut out the circle and decorate the door hanger.

Say • What do you usually hang these on? Door hangers usually invite guests to enter or not enter a room. In today's story, God's people used another type of sign to keep away an unwanted visitor.

Transition to large group

God Formed His Nation

Large Group LEADER

Session Title: The Passover
Bible Passage: Exodus 11:1–13:16
Big Picture Question: Why is the Passover important? The Passover was the way God chose to save His people and is a picture of Christ's sacrifice for sinners.
Key Passage: Exodus 6:7
Unit Christ Connection: God saved His people from physical captivity in Egypt as He would one day send Jesus to save His people from spiritual captivity.

• countdown video

Countdown

Show the countdown video as your kids arrive, and set it to end as large group time begins.

• any small brush

Introduce the session (1 minute)

[Large group leader enters with a small brush.]
Leader • I have a brush with me today. What do you think of when you see a brush? Probably paint. What else do you use a brush for? How about for brushing your hair or teeth? An archaeologist uses a brush, too. When an archaeologist has found something in the dirt, she puts down the shovel and picks up a brush. Why would she do that? She brushes away the dirt. She never just keeps digging because things that are really old are usually very fragile. She is just trying to protect what she found.

• Timeline Map

Timeline map (1 minute)

Leader • As we make our way through the Bible, we will find lots of times that God protected His people. That's what He was doing in our last two weeks of study.

Let's check out our timeline map. Remember how God protected baby Moses from the mean Pharaoh who was killing all the baby boys? When Moses grew up, God asked him through the burning bush to face Pharaoh and demand he let God's people go. Moses did as God asked. God showed Pharaoh, the Egyptians, and the Israelites that He was the one true God by sending nine plagues. Still, Pharaoh would not let God's people go to worship Him. But God wasn't done yet.

Big picture question (1 minute)

Leader • One of the ways we worship God is by reading His Word. How many of you have your Bible today? We check every week because it's important for you to have your Bible. The story of Moses is just one of the many true stories that helps us learn about who God is and how He sent Jesus to save us. So, if you have your Bible, hold it up. That's awesome!

Today's story is going to be one that will make you want to brush everything aside and listen closely. Let's explore our big picture question. ***Why is the Passover important?***

• "You Lift Me Up"

Sing (5 minutes)

Leader • Passover is a holiday that Jews today celebrate about the same time we celebrate Easter. In New Testament time, Jesus was crucified during the time of Passover. We will learn more about Passover in just a moment. The Bible all connects perfectly to tell of the One who lifts us up—Jesus.

Sing together "You Lift Me Up."

Key passage (4 minutes)

• "I Am Yahweh!"
• Key Passage Slide or Poster (enhanced CD)

Leader • God was not done after nine plagues against Egypt. God would, like always, keep His promise to make the Israelites His people.

Show the slide or poster of this unit's key passage, Exodus 6:7. Lead the boys and girls to read the verse together.

Leader • We are about to see God keep His promise. This promise that God made passed on to us many years later. When we know and love Jesus, we become God's people, too. Let's sing our key passage song.

Sing together "I Am Yahweh!"

Tell the Bible story (10 minutes)

• "The Passover" video
• Bibles, 1 per kid
• Bible Story Picture Slide or Poster (enhanced CD)

Leader • It's time to look into God's Word and find out the answer to our big picture question. *Why is the Passover important?*

Open your Bible to Exodus 11. Choose to tell the Bible story in your own words using the script provided, or show the "The Passover" video.

Leader • God had one more plague or punishment for Egypt. God would prove that all the fake gods the Egyptians worshiped were nothing and God was the one true God. All the firstborn Egyptian sons would die. God was still protecting His people though. God told every Israelite family to take a perfect lamb, kill it, and put its blood on their doorposts. God asked the Israelites to make a special meal using the lamb and unleavened bread, kind of like an unsalted cracker. They had to eat quickly because Pharaoh was about to let them go. After all the firstborn children died, including Pharaoh's son, God kept His promise. God's people were free. Every year, as God commanded, Jews still celebrate what God did that day during a weeklong celebration called Passover.

Ask the following review questions:

1. What was the tenth and final plague? (*death of the firstborn, Exodus 11:4-5*)

2. What animal did God tell His people to sacrifice? (*a lamb or goat, Exodus 12:5*)

3. Where were the Israelites told to put the blood from the lamb they had sacrificed? (*on their doorposts, Exodus 12:7*)

4. Did Pharaoh finally let the Israelites go? (*yes, Exodus 12:31-32*)

5. Who died and gave His blood so we could be free from sin? (*Jesus*)

Discussion starter video (4 minutes)

• "Lord's Supper" video

Leader • Christians don't celebrate Passover, but there is one part of the Passover meal that is very special. Watch this video.

Play "Lord's Supper."

Leader • How many of you have ever taken part in the Lord's Supper? Jesus celebrated the Passover meal with the disciples just hours before His trial and death on the cross. Jesus used the bread and juice from the Passover meal to begin a new tradition for people who believe that Jesus is the Son of God. The bread represents Jesus' body and the juice represents His blood, which saves us. The Bible tells us Jesus is the Lamb of God who takes away the sin of the world. We don't need to kill animals anymore because Jesus is the true sacrifice. ***Why is the Passover important? The Passover was the way God chose to save His people and is a picture of Christ's sacrifice for sinners.*** Those who trust in Jesus' sacrifice are protected by His blood from the punishment for sin.

The Gospel: God's Plan for Me (optional)

Use Scripture and the guide provided with this session to explain to boys and girls how to become a Christian. Assign individuals to meet with kids who have more questions. If this is not possible, encourage boys and girls to ask their parents, small group leaders, and other Christian adults any questions they may have about becoming a Christian.

• Big Picture Question
Slide or Poster
(enhanced CD)

Prayer (4 minutes)

Show the big picture question slide or poster.

Leader • This was a tough big picture question to answer with a long answer. Does anyone have a guess? *Why is the Passover important? The Passover was the way God chose to save His people and is a picture of Christ's sacrifice for sinners.*

Repeat the big picture question and answer several times. Challenge the kids to ask you the question, and you answer. Reverse roles and ask them the question, letting them answer.

Before transitioning to small group, make any necessary announcements. Lead the kids in prayer. Thank God for sending Jesus, the Lamb of God, and pray that kids will see that God still saves His people through Jesus.

Dismiss to small groups

The Gospel: God's Plan for Me

Ask kids if they have ever heard the word *gospel*. Clarify that the word *gospel* means "good news." It is the message about Christ, the kingdom of God, and salvation. Use the following guide to share the gospel with kids.

God rules. Explain to kids that the Bible tells us God created everything, and He is in charge of everything. Invite a volunteer to read Genesis 1:1 from the Bible. Read Revelation 4:11 or Colossians 1:16-17 aloud and explain what these verses mean.

We sinned. Tell kids that since the time of Adam and Eve, everyone has chosen to disobey God (Romans 3:23). The Bible calls this sin. Because God is holy, God cannot be around sin. Sin separates us from God and deserves God's punishment of death (Romans 6:23).

God provided. Choose a child to read John 3:16 aloud. Say that God sent His Son Jesus, the perfect solution to our sin problem, to rescue us from the punishment we deserve. It's something we, as sinners, could never earn on our own. Jesus alone saves us. Read and explain Ephesians 2:8-9.

Jesus gives. Share with kids that Jesus lived a perfect life, died on the cross for our sins, and rose again. Because Jesus gave up His life for us, we can be welcomed into God's family for eternity. This is the best gift ever! Read Romans 5:8; 2 Corinthians 5:21; or 1 Peter 3:18.

We respond. Tell kids that they can respond to Jesus. Read Romans 10:9-10,13. Review these aspects of our response: Believe in your heart that Jesus alone saves you through what He's already done on the cross. Repent, turning from self and sin to Jesus. Tell God and others that your faith is in Jesus.

Offer to talk with any child who is interested in responding to Jesus.

Small Group LEADER

Session Title: The Passover
Bible Passage: Exodus 11:1–13:16
Big Picture Question: Why is the Passover important? The Passover was the way God chose to save His people and is a picture of Christ's sacrifice for sinners.
Key Passage: Exodus 6:7
Unit Christ Connection: God saved His people from physical captivity in Egypt as He would one day send Jesus to save His people from spiritual captivity.

- Key Passage Slide or Poster (enhanced CD)
- dry erase board and markers (optional)

Key passage activity (5 minutes)

Make sure the key passage, Exodus 6:7, is visible for each child, either as the printed poster or written on a dry erase board. Read the verse together.

Say • Today we saw how God kept His promise to show the Israelites that they were His people and He was their God. After more than 400 years as slaves in Egypt, the people walked away free. They came to Egypt as a group of 70. They were just Jacob's family, saved from a famine by Joseph, but they left Egypt with 600,000 men and their families. They had become a nation. Remember the covenant God gave Abraham back in Genesis? They had become as numerous as the stars in the sky.

Instruct the kids to form a long single-file line. Lead the group in marching around the room. Tell them they are going to be like the Israelites leaving Egypt as an army. Only, they have to say a word of the key verse with each step until the verse is complete. Repeat walking faster. Next time, march slow, then fast, then slow.

Bible story review (10 minutes)

- Bibles, 1 per kid
- Small Group Visual Pack
- Big Picture Question Slide or Poster (enhanced CD)
- flour
- sugar
- salt
- shortening
- milk
- measuring cup
- bowl
- sifter
- spoon
- rolling pin
- knife
- sheet pan

Encourage the kids to find Exodus 11 in their Bibles. Help them as needed.

Say • Which book tells us how God rescued His people from Egypt? (*Exodus*) Is Exodus in the Old or New Testament? (*Old*) Exodus is part of which division of the Bible? (*Law*)

Use the small group visual pack to show kids where today's Bible story is on the timeline. Review the Bible story provided or summarize the story in your own words. As you review the story, lead the kids in helping you make unleavened bread. The recipe and instructions are below:

- 1 cup of plain flour
- 3 tablespoons of sugar
- ½ teaspoon of salt
- 1/3 cup of shortening
- 2–2½ tablespoons of milk

1. Sift flour, sugar, and salt.
2. Cut in shortening.
3. Add small amounts of milk until the dough is formed; discard remaining milk.
4. Roll the dough to ¼ inch thick.
5. Cut in ½ inch squares.
6. Bake at 375 degrees 15–20 minutes.

Because of the time to bake, make some ahead of time or purchase unleavened bread at a local grocery store. Share the pre-made or purchased bread with the kids.

Show the big picture question slide or poster.

Say • What do you think of the Passover bread? Do you remember our big picture question and answer. *Why is the Passover important? The Passover was the way God chose to save His people and is a picture of Christ's sacrifice for sinners.*

God Formed His Nation

Activity choice (10 minutes)

Option 1: Color code

Spread several different pieces of colored construction paper or other colored paper throughout the room. Give the kids 30 seconds to find a color and stand on or near it. When the 30 seconds are over, call out one of the colors. Those standing on the color you call are the winners.

• construction paper, various colors

Say • The Israelites only had one way to escape the judgment meant for the Egyptians. They had to sacrifice a perfect lamb and put the lamb's blood around their door. This became known as Passover. *Why is the Passover important? The Passover was the way God chose to save His people and is a picture of Christ's sacrifice for sinners.*

Option 2: Door frame

• heavyweight paper
• large craft sticks, 2 per kid
• regular craft sticks, 2 per kid
• glue
• crayons or markers

Provide a piece of heavyweight paper, two large craft sticks, and two regular craft sticks. Demonstrate how to place the two large craft sticks vertically on the heavyweight paper with one regular craft stick at the top and one at the bottom. This will create a rectangle. Tell the kids to glue the regular craft sticks completely but only the outer edges of the large craft sticks. Encourage the kids to color the sticks so that it looks like a door. Trim the excess heavyweight paper. Add additional decorations if you choose. A trimmed 5-by-7-inch landscape photo should fit in the frame. Tuck the picture under the large craft sticks.

Say • Because the Israelites obeyed God's command to place the blood of a perfect lamb or goat on their doors, they were protected from the final plague on Egypt. We are protected from the plague of sin when we trust in Jesus as our Savior and Lord. *Why is the Passover important? The Passover was the way God* *chose to save His people and is a picture of Christ's sacrifice for sinners.*

- folder, 1 per kid
- Journal Page, 1 per kid (enhanced CD)
- markers or crayons
- Bible Story Coloring Page

Journal and Prayer (5 minutes)

Distribute each child's journal and the journal page provided with this session. Instruct the kids to draw a picture of elements of the Lord's Supper. Older kids can write what each element represents.

Say • Let's take one last look at our big picture question. *Why is the Passover important? The Passover was the way God chose to save His people and is a picture of Christ's sacrifice for sinners.*

Make sure each child puts this week's sheet in his journal then collect them. Keep the journals in the classroom so they will be available every week or as often as you wish to use them.

If time remains, take prayer requests or allow kids to color the coloring page provided with this session. End the session with prayer, thanking God for giving Jesus as our sacrifice. Pray for each child by name, and ask God to help each kid understand the sacrifice made for him.

Teacher BIBLE STUDY

The crossing of the Red Sea is an event in history that exudes God's grace. This even has been remembered for generations as God's mighty redemptive act. God had clearly shown His power in Egypt through the 10 plagues; at the Red Sea, God acted in an even mightier way.

Instead of leading the Israelites into the wilderness, God instructed Moses to turn back so that the Egyptians would think they were lost. God purposefully hardened Pharaoh's heart so that he would pursue the Israelites. Why? "Then I will receive glory by means of Pharaoh and all his army, and the Egyptians will know that I am Yahweh" (Ex. 14:4).

Imagine the fear the Israelites felt as they saw the Egyptians pursuing them. They expressed it in their complaints to Moses. (See Ex. 14:11.) Moses spoke up to calm them: "The LORD will fight for you" (Ex. 14:14).

The LORD did fight for them. All night long, the LORD kept a pillar of a cloud between Egypt's chariots and the Israelites. Then He instructed Moses to stretch out his hand; God drove back the sea with a powerful east wind. By faith, the Israelites passed through on dry ground! (See Hebrews 11:29.) When Pharaoh and the Egyptians followed after them, the waters came back and covered the entire army of Pharaoh. None of them survived.

As you teach kids this week, help them understand that God helps people who love Him. He also punishes sin. God created a way to save His chosen people by parting the Red Sea. In the same way, God created the way for people to escape the penalty of sin through His Son, Jesus Christ. God didn't make the way of salvation for us because we deserve it, but because of who He is: a gracious and loving God who created us to be in relationship with Himself.

Younger Kids BIBLE STUDY OVERVIEW

Session Title: The Israelites Crossed the Red Sea

Bible Passage: Exodus 13:17–17:7

Big Picture Question: Is anything too hard for God to do? Nothing is impossible for God.

Key Passage: Exodus 6:7

Unit Christ Connection: God saved His people from physical captivity in Egypt as He would one day send Jesus to save His people from spiritual captivity.

God Formed His Nation

The BIBLE STORY

The Israelites Crossed the Red Sea
Exodus 13:17–17:7

After the tenth plague, the Israelites quickly left Egypt. The LORD led the people toward the Red Sea and the wilderness. As they traveled, the LORD went ahead of them in a pillar of cloud to lead them during the day. At night, God was in a pillar of fire to give them light, so they could travel by day or by night. God told Moses to have the people camp near the sea. God said that Pharaoh would change his mind and pursue the Israelites. God wanted to prove to the Israelites that He is God.

Pharaoh and his officials did change their minds. Pharaoh got in his chariot and took his troops with him. He pursued the Israelites, and they caught up with them where they were camping near the sea.

The Israelites saw the Egyptians coming and they were afraid. "We are going to die!" they said. "We should have never left Egypt!"

But Moses said, "Do not be afraid. God brought you here, and He will fight for you. You will never see the Egyptians again."

God told Moses what to do: "Stretch out your hand over the sea, and divide it so that the Israelites can go through the sea on dry ground." Then God moved behind the Israelites to hold back the Egyptians for the night. In the morning, Moses stretched out his hand and divided the sea. The Israelites walked through with walls of water on both sides.

The Egyptians went after them. As soon as the Israelites were safely on the other side of the sea, Moses stretched out his hand again and the waters returned, covering the Egyptians and killing all of Pharaoh's army. None of them survived.

When the Israelites saw what had happened, they feared God and believed that He had sent Moses to lead them.

Moses and the Israelites sang a song to the LORD. "The LORD is my strength and my song," they said. "He has become my salvation."

Moses led the people away from the Red Sea, and they came to the wilderness. They could not find good water to drink, and they complained to Moses. God said, "If you obey Me and do what is right and keep My commands, I will not treat you like I treated the Egyptians. I am Yahweh, who heals you." The Israelites came to a place called Elim (EE lim) where there was plenty of food and water. They camped there.

The Israelites left Elim and journeyed into the wilderness. They were hungry. They complained to Moses. "We were better off living in Egypt!" they said. "You brought us out here to die!" But Moses had not brought them out there to die. God knew what He was doing.

God said, "I have heard the complaints of the Israelites. Tell them: At twilight you will eat meat, and in the morning you will eat bread until you are full. Then you will know that I am Yahweh your God."

So at evening, quail came into the camp. In the morning, fine flakes like frost were on the ground. "What is it?" the Israelites asked. Moses said, "It is the bread the LORD has given you to eat." The Israelites called it *manna*, which means "what is it?" They collected just enough to eat for the day. If they collected too much, the leftovers went bad. On the sixth day, they collected twice as much because the seventh day was the Sabbath; no one collected any manna on the Sabbath. The Israelites ate manna for 40 years, until they came to the border of the land of Canaan (KAY nuhn).

The Israelites moved about the wilderness as the Lord told them to do. One day they came to a camp with no water. "Give us something to drink," they told Moses. "Why are you complaining to me?" Moses asked. "You brought us out here to die" the Israelites said. They forgot that the Lord had a plan for them.

"Lord, what should I do?" Moses cried out. God showed Moses a rock and instructed him to hit it with his staff. Water came out of it, and the people drank. It was a sign that the Lord was with them.

Christ Connection: God created a way for the Israelites to escape the Egyptians. In the same way, God created the way for people to escape the penalty of sin—His Son, Jesus Christ. Jesus is the only way to get to God.

Small Group OPENING

Session Title: The Israelites Crossed the Red Sea
Bible Passage: Exodus 13:17–17:7
Big Picture Question: Is anything too hard for God to do? Nothing is impossible for God.
Key Passage: Exodus 6:7
Unit Christ Connection: God saved His people from physical captivity in Egypt as He would one day send Jesus to save His people from spiritual captivity.

Welcome time

Arriving Activity: Crossing guard

Select a volunteer to be a crossing guard. Group the kids so that kids stand to the guard's right and left, along with some in front. Those to the left and right must act like cars passing in front of the guard. When the guard holds up a hand, each line of traffic must stop and let the kids in front of him walk safely across. The guard will then wave the cars to continue driving. Continue with a new crossing guard.

Say • Today, we will learn about how God stopped a sea from flowing when one man put his hand up.

Activity page (5 minutes)

• "Moses' Life" activity page, 1 per kid
• pencils

Guide boys and girls to complete the activity page.

Say • God took Moses from a basket on the Nile to a leader of a nation, but God wasn't through using Moses. We'll see more in today's session.

Session starter (10 minutes)

Option 1: Moses, May I?

Choose a volunteer to be "Moses," and position him near a

wall. Line up the other kids to face Moses from the opposite wall. Moses chooses one of the kids and says something like, "Bobby, you may take five small steps." The kid who was addressed then responds, "Moses, may I?" Moses then says, "Yes, you may," or "No, but you may take three small steps." The kid Moses asks must always follow a response from Moses with "Moses, may I?" She may not move from her spot unless Moses says, "Yes, you may." Moses then addresses another kid, and the game continues until one of the kids reaches Moses. Whoever makes it to Moses first becomes Moses for the next round. If a kid moves without Moses' permission or doesn't follow Moses' instructions, he must start back at the beginning. Change out Moses every minute to keep the game moving.

Say • Moses led God's people out of Egypt, but one more thing would stand in their way. We'll find out what in just a few minutes.

Option 2: Collecting manna

• several paperclips, marshmallows, or other small items

Toss several paper clips, marshmallows, or other small items throughout the room. Tell the kids you need them to collect the items as quickly as possible. Give a signal for go. Once kids collect all the items, let them count to see who found the most. Invite the kids to scatter the items throughout the room again. Repeat the game. This time choose a number between 1 and 20. The winner will be the one who gathers closest to that number. Don't share the winning number until the "manna" has been collected.

Say • The Israelites left Egypt and soon found that living on their own wasn't always easy, but God had a plan to take care of His people.

Transition to large group

Large Group LEADER

Session Title: The Israelites Crossed the Red Sea
Bible Passage: Exodus 13:17–17:7
Big Picture Question: Is anything too hard for God to do? Nothing is impossible for God.
Key Passage: Exodus 6:7
Unit Christ Connection: God saved His people from physical captivity in Egypt as He would one day send Jesus to save His people from spiritual captivity.

• countdown video

Countdown

Show the countdown video as your kids arrive, and set it to end as large group time begins.

• map

Introduce the session (1 minute)

[Large group leader enters with a map, looking around like she is lost.]

Leader • Do any of you know how to read a map? I bet your parents use a GPS or an online map. Believe it or not, a map is an important tool for an archaeologist. Archaeologists use old maps and new maps to try to find whatever they are looking for. After all, you can't dig for something if you don't know where to start digging! If you remember last week, God's people—the Israelites— left Egypt. Now, where would they go? How would they know where to go?

• Timeline Map

Timeline map (1 minute)

Leader • Let's find out where they were going by looking at our map, the timeline map. The timeline map helps us see when and where all the true stories in the Bible happened and how the Bible all fits together. Here's where we were last week, "The Passover." Today we are learning that "The Israelites Crossed the Red Sea." Wow, crossing a sea. That must take a really big boat or a large bridge. Maybe they took an airplane. What do you think?

Big picture question (1 minute)

Leader • We have only one place we can go to find the answer. The Bible has all the answers from the real stories we learn about. More importantly, the Bible teaches us about God and how everything points to Jesus coming to save us. If you have your Bible with you today, hold it high.

Let's get going on today's journey. First, we need to see our big picture question. *Is anything too hard for God to do?*

Sing (5 minutes)

• "You Lift Me Up" song

Leader • Lots of things are too hard for me. I even struggle to read this map. Is anything too hard for you? Moses thought facing Pharaoh would be impossible; however, God had plans to take Moses and lift him up to do amazing things.

Sing together "You Lift Me Up."

Key passage (4 minutes)

• "I Am Yahweh!" song
• Key Passage Slide or Poster (enhanced CD)

Leader • Last week, God protected the Israelites from the final plague. All they had to do was obey His instructions. This act was one of the ways God chose to prove He was their God.

Show the slide or poster of this unit's key passage, Exodus 6:7. Lead the boys and girls to read the verse together.

Leader • We saw God keep His promise once again when the Israelites left Egypt. God said He would be their God. We can hold onto that promise, too. We can celebrate God when we repent of our sin and trust in Jesus. Let's sing our key passage to Him.

Sing together "I Am Yahweh!"

Tell the Bible story (10 minutes)

• "The Israelites Crossed the Red Sea" video
• Bibles, 1 per kid
• Bible Story Picture Slide or Poster (enhanced CD)

Leader • We are about to see how God proved over and over that the Israelites were His people. Let's see what happened after God's people left Egypt and find the answer to our big picture question. *Is anything too hard for God to do?*

Open your Bible to Exodus 13. Choose to tell the Bible story in your own words using the script provided, or show the "The Israelites Crossed the Red Sea" video.

Leader • Wow! Can you imagine seeing this sea in front of you and an army coming from behind you? The Israelites thought it would be impossible to escape. But they had a God who could do anything. *Is anything too hard for God to do? Nothing is impossible for God.* Imagine the sea splitting right in front of you. You walk across on dry land with walls of water on both sides. Finally, God takes out the mean army coming after you with those same waters. That should have been proof for the Israelites that God was going to take care of them and that nothing was impossible for Him. It wasn't. It wasn't long before they were complaining about not having enough food and water. Still, God performed a miracle each time, proving He can do anything.

Ask the following review questions:

1. What did God use to lead His people once they left Egypt? (*a pillar of cloud by day and fire by*

night, Exodus 13:21-22)

2. What happened to the Red Sea when Moses first raised his hand? (*It parted and the Israelites walked through on dry land, Exodus 14:21-22*)

3. What happened to the Egyptian army? (*God drowned them in the sea, Exodus 14:28*)

4. God split the Red Sea, so His people could escape. What does Jesus provide the way for us to escape from? (*sin, God's judgment*)

Discussion starter video (4 minutes)

• "That's Impossible" video

Leader • Have you ever faced something that seemed impossible? Maybe something like this has happened to you.

Play "That's Impossible."

Leader • What is impossible for us is not impossible for God. ***Is anything too hard for God to do? Nothing is impossible for God.*** The Israelites needed a way to escape the Egyptian army, so God divided the Red Sea. To us, sin is like the Red Sea. It is impossible for us to be with God because we sin, and God is holy. However, ***nothing is impossible for God.*** He sent Jesus to live a life without sin, so we could be with God once again.

The Gospel: God's Plan for Me (optional)

Use Scripture and the guide provided with this session to explain to boys and girls how to become a Christian. Assign individuals to meet with kids who have more questions. If this is not possible, encourage boys and girls to ask their parents, small group leaders, and other Christian adults any questions they may have about becoming a Christian.

Prayer (4 minutes)

Show the big picture question slide or poster.

Leader • Who would like to volunteer to answer our big picture question? *Is anything too hard for God to do? Nothing is impossible for God.*

Ask for a volunteer. Invite the volunteer to ask the question and then challenge another kid by name to give the answer. The kid who gives the answer then challenges another kid. Repeat as time allows.

Before transitioning to small group, make any necessary announcements. Lead the kids in prayer. Thank God for providing ways out of things that sometimes seem impossible to us, and pray that kids will know and trust that God is able to do all things.

Dismiss to small groups

The Gospel: God's Plan for Me

Ask kids if they have ever heard the word *gospel*. Clarify that the word *gospel* means "good news." It is the message about Christ, the kingdom of God, and salvation. Use the following guide to share the gospel with kids.

God rules. Explain to kids that the Bible tells us God created everything, and He is in charge of everything. Invite a volunteer to read Genesis 1:1 from the Bible. Read Revelation 4:11 or Colossians 1:16-17 aloud and explain what these verses mean.

We sinned. Tell kids that since the time of Adam and Eve, everyone has chosen to disobey God (Romans 3:23). The Bible calls this sin. Because God is holy, God cannot be around sin. Sin separates us from God and deserves God's punishment of death (Romans 6:23).

God provided. Choose a child to read John 3:16 aloud. Say that God sent His Son Jesus, the perfect solution to our sin problem, to rescue us from the punishment we deserve. It's something we, as sinners, could never earn on our own. Jesus alone saves us. Read and explain Ephesians 2:8-9.

Jesus gives. Share with kids that Jesus lived a perfect life, died on the cross for our sins, and rose again. Because Jesus gave up His life for us, we can be welcomed into God's family for eternity. This is the best gift ever! Read Romans 5:8; 2 Corinthians 5:21; or 1 Peter 3:18.

We respond. Tell kids that they can respond to Jesus. Read Romans 10:9-10,13. Review these aspects of our response: Believe in your heart that Jesus alone saves you through what He's already done on the cross. Repent, turning from self and sin to Jesus. Tell God and others that your faith is in Jesus.

Offer to talk with any child who is interested in responding to Jesus.

Small Group LEADER

Session Title: The Israelites Crossed the Red Sea
Bible Passage: Exodus 13:17–17:7
Big Picture Question: Is anything too hard for God to do? Nothing is impossible for God.
Key Passage: Exodus 6:7
Unit Christ Connection: God saved His people from physical captivity in Egypt as He would one day send Jesus to save His people from spiritual captivity.

- Key Passage Slide or Poster (enhanced CD)
- dry erase board and markers (optional)
- marker
- index cards

Key passage activity (5 minutes)

Make sure the key passage, Exodus 6:7, is visible for each child, either as the printed poster or written on a dry erase board. Read the verse together.

Say • Today we learned how God continued to provide for His people, the Israelites. God proved His promise to be their God time and time again. He led them with a cloud in the day and fire at night. He divided the Red Sea and brought them safely through the middle and washed away their enemy. He gave them food from heaven and gave them water from a rock when they needed it.

While all those things were impossible for the people, they were not for God. *Is anything too hard for God to do? Nothing is impossible for God.*

Write the key passage on a set of any size index cards with three or four words per card. Make three sets. Designate three groups and let them race to see who can put a set in order the fastest.

Bible story review (10 minutes)

• Bibles, 1 per kid
• Small Group Visual Pack
• Big Picture Question Slide or Poster (enhanced CD)

Encourage the kids to find Exodus 13 in their Bibles. Help them as needed.

Say • How many books are there in the Bible? (*66*) What number is Exodus? (*2*) Is Exodus in the Old or New Testament? (*Old*) Exodus is part of which division of the Bible? (*Law*)

Use the small group visual pack to show kids where today's Bible story is on the timeline. Review the Bible story provided or summarize the story in your own words. As you review the story, choose groups of kids to make sound effects. Direct the kids by pointing to the right group as you tell the story. Instruct them to only make their noise when you point to them. Use the ideas below, or come up with your own.

- Red Sea - making a "sh" sound
- Egyptian army - stomping fast
- Israelites fussing - saying "no" continuously
- Manna - saying, "What is it?"
- Water - making a "gulp" sound

Show the big picture question slide or poster.

Say • We may be able to make sounds of the events that really happened, but only God could have made those events real. Only He can do the impossible. *Is anything too hard for God to do? Nothing is impossible for God.*

Activity choice (10 minutes)

Option 1: Water game

Tape two 6-foot parallel lines about a foot apart. If you have more room, tape longer lines. Tape a start line about a foot from the bottom of the lines. Encourage the kids to line up behind the start line. Choose a volunteer. The volunteer

• tape

must face away from the lines. The volunteer raises her hand. When she does, kids can pass between the lines. The Red Sea is "parted." If the volunteer drops her hand, anyone still between the taped lines is out. Any kid who steps on or outside of the lines is immediately out. Once a kid goes through the "sea," he may return to the end of the line and go through again. Allow the volunteer to hold up her hand and drop her hand several times. Choose another volunteer and play again. Repeat as time allows.

Say • Moses raised his hand over the sea and it divided, but God was the one who parted it. God can do what is impossible for us. *Is anything too hard for God to do? Nothing is impossible for God.*

Option 2: 3-D sea

- brown, gray, or black construction paper, 1 per kid
- blue construction paper, 1 per kid
- scissors, 1 per kid
- glue
- crayons or markers
- O-shaped cereal or small candies (optional)
- fish-shaped crackers or fish-shaped candy (optional)
- ziplock bag (optional)

Give each child two sheets of construction paper, one brown, gray, or black and one light blue. He can cut the blue sheet in half, lengthwise or widthwise. This will be the sea, so kids can cut it out with waves. It doesn't have to be perfect. Fold the blue halves in half again and glue the uncut edges to the matching edges of the darker sheet. This will be the sea floor. The cut edges should stand up to represent walls of water. Kids can draw people crossing the sea, or they can sprinkle O-shaped cereal or small candies to represent people between the walls of water. They may also draw fish or sprinkle fish-shaped crackers or candy on the sea. Provide a ziplock bag if you provide snack items.

Say • Dividing the Red Sea was just one thing God did to prove He could and would do the impossible for His people. *Is anything too hard for God to do? Nothing is impossible for God.*

Journal and Prayer (5 minutes)

- folder, 1 per kid
- Journal Page, 1 per kid (enhanced CD)
- markers or crayons
- Bible Story Coloring page

Distribute each child's journal and the journal page provided with this session. Instruct the kids to draw a picture of what they think manna might have looked like. Older kids can write the big picture question and answer.

Say • Here's one more look at our big picture question. *Is anything too hard for God to do? Nothing is impossible for God.*

Make sure each child puts this week's sheet in his journal and collect them. Keep the journals in the classroom so they will be available every week or as often as you wish to use them.

If time remains, take prayer requests or allow kids to color the coloring page provided with this session. End the session with prayer, thanking God for making the impossible possible. Pray for each child by name, and ask God to help each kid have faith that God can do what we can't.

Unit 6: THE WILDERNESS

Big Picture Questions

Session 1: Why did God give His people the Ten Commandments? God is holy and wants His people to be holy.

Session 2: What does the tabernacle show about God? God wants to dwell with His people and be worshiped by them.

Session 3: Why did God require a blood sacrifice? Because God is holy, His forgiveness requires a payment for sin. Jesus made the ultimate payment for sin with His death on the cross.

Session 4: What happens when God's people sin? Sin has a price, but God forgives when people seek forgiveness.

Session 5: What happens when people repent from sin? Sin comes with consequences, but God provides the way of salvation.

Session 6: Who protected God's people? God protected His people from their enemies.

Unit 6: THE WILDERNESS

Unit Description: The Israelite nation, freshly saved from Egyptian taskmasters, continued to grumble and complain against God and His chosen leader, Moses. Even though God's people rebelled against Him, He never forgot the promise He first gave to Abraham. God never changes. Wilderness wanderings signify the life Christians today live when they don't fully commit themselves to following God's plan and instruction.

Unit Key Passage: Exodus 20:1-17

Unit Christ Connection: God instructed His covenant people how to live holy lives in an unholy world. This sustained their relationship with God until the perfect plan was revealed through Jesus Christ.

Session 1: God Gave the Ten Commandments
Exodus 19:1–20:21; 31:18; 32:1-35; 34:1-9

Session 2: The Tabernacle Was Built
Exodus 35:4–40:38

Session 3: God Gave Rules for Sacrifice
Leviticus 1–27

Session 4: Joshua and Caleb
Numbers 13:1–14:38

Session 5: The Bronze Snake
Numbers 17:1-12; 20:1-12,14-20; 21:4-9

Session 6: Balaam
Numbers 22:1–24:25

Teacher BIBLE STUDY

God rescued His people from the Egyptians! He then led them into the desert toward Mount Sinai. The Israelites camped at the base of the mountain while Moses went up the mountain to talk to God. God gave Moses the laws the Israelites were to obey. God renewed the covenant He made with Abraham, Isaac, and Jacob with the whole nation of Israel. They were His people, and He was their God. (Ex. 19:5-6)

God wanted perfect obedience in response to His rescuing the Israelites from slavery in Egypt. His laws covered every part of their lives, and the laws were summed up in the Ten Commandments. God did not give laws just for the sake of having laws. His laws had a purpose; they revealed to the people what life will be like when Christ establishes His kingdom. They showed how righteous people live and interact with God and with others.

The Ten Commandments can be grouped into two categories: the first four laws deal with a person's relationship to God and the last six laws deal with a person's relationship to others.

Just 10. It would be easy enough to keep just 10 rules, right? The Israelites proved they could not keep a single one of God's laws. Their hearts were full of sin. Moses mediated for the Israelites, asking God to forgive the people's sin. Moses was a good mediator, but he wasn't perfect. The Israelites needed someone who could keep the laws perfectly for them, mediate between them and God, and satisfy God's wrath against them. They needed Jesus.

The kids you teach this week have sinful hearts. They cannot obey God perfectly, and they need a Savior. Point kids to Jesus and help them understand that God is pleased with us because He looks at Jesus, who never sinned. Because of Christ, we can have a right relationship with God.

Younger Kids BIBLE STUDY OVERVIEW

Session Title: God Gave the Ten Commandments
Bible Passage: Exodus 19:1–20:21; 31:18; 32:1-35; 34:1-9
Big Picture Question: Why did God give His people the Ten
Commandments? God is holy and wants His people to be holy.
Key Passage: Exodus 20:1-17
Unit Christ Connection: God instructed His covenant people how to live
holy lives in an unholy world. This sustained their relationship with God
until the perfect plan was revealed through Jesus Christ.

Small Group Opening

Large Group Leader

Small Group Leader

The BIBLE STORY

God Gave the Ten Commandments
Exodus 19:1–20:21; 31:18; 32:1-35; 34:1-9

Three months after the Israelites left Egypt, they came into the Wilderness of Sinai (SIGH nigh). They camped in front of the mountain. God had a plan to make the Israelites His special people. Moses went up the mountain to God. God called to him from the mountain: "This is what you should tell the Israelites: 'You have seen what I did to the Egyptians and how I rescued you and brought you to Me. If you listen carefully to Me and you keep My covenant, you will be My people.'" God was making a covenant with the people.

Moses went back to the people and told them what God had said. They agreed on the covenant. All the people responded together, "We will do all that the LORD has spoken." So Moses went back to talk to God.

"I am going to come to you in a dense cloud," God explained. "I want the people to hear Me speak to you, so that they will believe you." Moses got the people ready. On the third day, thunder and lightning rumbled! A thick cloud came upon the mountain, and a loud trumpet sounded. Everyone in the camp shuddered. Then Moses brought the people out of the camp to meet God, and they stood at the foot of the mountain.

God came down the mountain in a fire, and smoke covered the mountain. The mountain shook and the sound of the trumpet got louder and louder. God told the people not to come up the mountain. Then God gave Moses the Ten Commandments:

"I am the LORD your God, who brought you out of the land of Egypt, out of the place of slavery. Do not have other gods besides Me. Do not make an idol for yourself. Do not misuse the name of the LORD your God. Remember the Sabbath day, to keep it holy. Honor your father and your mother. Do not murder. Do not commit adultery. Do not steal. Do not give false testimony against your neighbor. Do not covet your neighbor's possessions."

The people heard God speaking to Moses, and they were afraid. They heard the law God gave them. "Let God talk to you," they said, "then tell us what He said. Do not let God speak to us, or we will die."

"Do not be afraid," Moses said. "God wants you to fear Him, so that you will not sin." The people stood still and Moses approached the thick darkness where God was. Moses was on the mountain for 40 days. When God was finished speaking to Moses on Mount Sinai, He gave him two stone tablets that God had written on with His own finger.

The Israelites, however, were getting impatient. Moses seemed to be on the mountain forever! Where was he? What was taking so long? "We need a god to lead us because we don't know where Moses is," they said. So the people made a gold calf that they could worship.

God told Moses what the people had done, and Moses rushed down the mountain. He carried the two stone tablets. When Moses got closer to the camp and saw that the people were dancing before the gold calf, he became very angry! He threw down the stone tablets, smashing them at the bottom of the mountain. Then he took the calf they made and destroyed it.

"What were you thinking?" Moses asked.

Moses saw that the people had sinned. He went up to talk to God. "Please forgive them," Moses said. God wanted to make the people pay for their sin, so He inflicted a plague on them.

God made Moses two more stone tablets to replace the ones Moses had broken. God spoke to Moses: "Yahweh is a compassionate and gracious God … but He will not leave the guilty unpunished."

Moses bowed down and worshiped God. "Lord, please go with us," he said. "Forgive our sin, and accept us as Your people."

Christ Connection: God made a covenant with His people: If you obey Me, you will be My people. (Exodus 19:5-6) But the people did not obey God. They sinned against God, and Moses asked God to forgive them. Moses acted as their mediator, or advocate, before God. When we sin, Jesus is our Mediator. Through Jesus, we are forgiven of our sins. God is pleased with us because He looks at Jesus, who never sinned.

Small Group OPENING

Session Title: God Gave the Ten Commandments
Bible Passage: Exodus 19:1–20:21; 31:18; 32:1-35; 34:1-9
Big Picture Question: Why did God give His people the Ten Commandments? God is holy and wants His people to be holy.
Key Passage: Exodus 20:1-17
Unit Christ Connection: God instructed His covenant people how to live holy lives in an unholy world. This sustained their relationship with God until the perfect plan was revealed through Jesus Christ.

Welcome time

Arriving Activity: Rules, rules

Engage kids in conversation as they enter the room. Ask the kids about rules they have at home and school.

Say • Share a rule you have at home or school.
• Do you like rules? Why or why not?
• What rule would you change if you could?

Activity page (5 minutes)

• "God's Commands" activity page, 1 per kid
• pencils

Guide boys and girls to complete the activity page.

Say • In this session, we are going to look at a set of rules God gave to the Israelites, and we will see if they were able to keep them.

Session starter (10 minutes)

Option 1: Numbers game

Group kids in pairs to form teams. Instruct each pair to face each other. On the count of three, everyone will throw one hand out with one to five fingers extended as if they are counting. Each pair will then count the number of fingers extended for their team. If one kid had two and the other had three, their total would be five. The leader should call out a number between one and ten. The winners are the pairs that have the exact number or the closest number to it.

Say • God asked His people, the Israelites, to follow 10 rules. Do you think they were able to follow them? We'll find out today.

Option 2: Which love?

- buckets, 2
- paper, 5 pieces
- marker
- tape

Tape a starting line and place two buckets a few feet away. Place a sign in front of one bucket that says, *Love God*. Place a sign in front of the other bucket that says, *Love Others*. Explain that in today's story God gave the Israelites 10 commands or rules. Each command tells us how we should and should not treat God, or how we should and should not treat others. Line up the kids single file behind the starting line. Give the first kid three paperwads. Read one of the Ten Commandments in any order, and encourage the kid to try to throw at least one of the paperwads in the correct bucket. Repeat with the next kid. Continue as time allows.

Say • Jesus tells us in the New Testament that all the commandments really come down to two rules: love God and love others.

Transition to large group

Large Group LEADER

Session Title: God Gave the Ten Commandments
Bible Passage: Exodus 19:1–20:21; 31:18; 32:1-35; 34:1-9
Big Picture Question: Why did God give His people the Ten Commandments? God is holy and wants His people to be holy.
Key Passage: Exodus 20:1-17
Unit Christ Connection: God instructed His covenant people how to live holy lives in an unholy world. This sustained their relationship with God until the perfect plan was revealed through Jesus Christ.

• room decorations

Suggested Theme Decorating Ideas: Create a desert scene using brown or tan flat sheets or other fabric. You may wish to place objects under the fabric to create dunes. Attach blue paper or a blue sheet to the wall behind the desert scene to create a sky. Place a few artificial or potted palm trees around a small blue pool to create an oasis on one side of the teaching area. Place stuffed animals that you might see in a desert, such as camels, snakes, lizards, turtles, and so forth. Post a sign on the wall stating "Camel Trek Tours this way" or a similar phrase.

• countdown video

Countdown

Show the countdown video as your kids arrive, and set it to end as large group time begins.

• long piece of paper

Introduce the session (1 minute)

[Large group leader enters with a long list.]

Leader • How many of you like rules? Can anyone give me a rule you have been told by a parent or teacher? Here is a list of possible rules: don't run in the house; don't yell; be nice to your sister; don't push; don't talk back. Those are just a few rules you have probably heard before.

Do you think rules are important? How about "look both ways before you cross the street"? The truth is rules are important because they usually protect us or others. "Don't run" because you might fall. "Be nice to your sister" because it shows love. Rules give us direction.

Timeline map (1 minute)

• Timeline Map

Leader • Imagine being the Israelites. They went out of slavery in Egypt and crossed the Red Sea where God destroyed the Egyptian army. They were now in the wilderness. They were free, but what now? Where would they go? What would they do? What did being God's people really mean? Well, let's answer some of those questions today, but we need to know where we are going first. Here we go. "God Gave the Ten Commandments." Who can tell me one of the Ten Commandments? God gave His people commands to follow for a reason.

Big picture question (1 minute)

Leader • God has a plan for everything. We may not always understand why some things happen, but God knows. We can understand His overall plan for us and our lives. That's why we have our Bibles.

If you have a Bible with you, let's see it. Alright, now let's find out what we will discover in our Bibles today. It's time for our big picture question. ***Why did God give His people the Ten Commandments?***

Sing (5 minutes)

• "Give You Glory" song

Leader • The Israelites had seen God do some amazing things, but they had no idea what was next. God used them to show the people of Egypt who He was, and God would continue to use them to show His greatness.

The stories in the Old Testament give us a clear picture of just how great our God is and a glimpse of His plan to send Jesus to die for us. Because of Jesus, we can give God glory.

Sing together "Give You Glory."

Key passage (4 minutes)

Leader • It made sense that God needed to give His people rules. These rules would help guide His people and keep them from sinning against God and others. Our key passage for the next several weeks is a list of those rules. Let's take a look at them.

Show the slides or posters of this unit's key passage, Exodus 20:1-17. Lead the boys and girls to read the key passage together.

Leader • I don't know if you have noticed, but the Ten Commandments tell God's people how they should treat God and how they should treat each other. The Israelites needed to know what it meant to be God's people. Ten rules doesn't sound like too much, does it? Let's see if we can try to remember them. Maybe this song will help.

Sing together "Ten Commandments."

Tell the Bible story (10 minutes)

Leader • Let's turn to the Bible to find out what happened while God was giving Moses the Ten Commandments and what happened after. Why don't we dig into God's Word and see more about this mighty God? As we look, remember our big picture question. *Why did God give His people the Ten Commandments?*

Open your Bible to Exodus 19. Choose to tell the Bible story in your own words using the script provided, or show the "God Gave the Ten Commandments" video.

- "Ten Commandments" song
- Key Passage Slides or Posters (enhanced CD)

- "God Gave the Ten Commandments" video
- Bibles, 1 per kid
- Bible Story Picture Slide or Poster (enhanced CD)

Leader • God promised the Israelites He would be their God. However, God is holy. He wanted them to understand that a relationship with Him required that they be holy, too. Because of this, He gave them rules to keep them from sinning. ***Why did God give His people the Ten Commandments? God is holy and wants His people to be holy.***

God told them how to treat Him. He said to worship Him and only Him, to take His name seriously, and to keep God's special day holy. Then He told them how to treat others. He said honor mom and dad, don't kill, don't cheat on a marriage promise, don't steal, don't lie about somebody, and don't wish you had someone else's stuff.

Just days later, as God was talking to Moses on a mountain, the people disobeyed the first two commandments by trying to make another god and then worshiping it! Even when they knew the rules, the Israelites still sinned. Moses went to God for the people to ask forgiveness.

We need someone like Moses, too. Romans 3:23 says we all sin, even though we know the rules. Jesus came to earth to live a holy life. When we repent and trust in Jesus as the sacrifice for our sins, He goes to God for us, and we are saved.

Ask the following review questions:

1. What was the name of the place where God's people camped months after leaving Egypt? (*Sinai, Exodus 19:1*)

2. What did God ask them to do as His people? (*keep His covenant or commands, Exodus 19:5*)

3. What did God write the Ten Commandments on? (*two stone tablets, Exodus 32:15-16*)

4. What were the people worshiping when Moses was

on the mountain? (*a calf, Exodus 32:3-6*)

5. How does Moses remind us of Jesus?
(*Moses sought forgiveness for the people, Exodus 32:11-15*)

Discussion starter video (4 minutes)

• "Rules, Rules" video

Leader • Have you ever been given rules that you did not obey? Maybe you feel like all anyone ever does is give you rules.

Play "Rules, Rules."

Leader • We have rules for a reason. Rules protect us and help us treat others fairly. God's rules to His people do that too, but God also had a bigger reason. ***Why did God give His people the Ten Commandments? God is holy and wants His people to be holy.*** The problem is that God's people couldn't be holy. They sinned just days after getting the commands. Moses had to go to God for the people and ask Him to forgive them. You and I are no different than the Israelites. We sin, too. We need someone to go to God for us. Jesus is that someone. He is holy and lived a holy life so He could go to God for us.

The Gospel: God's Plan for Me (optional)

Use Scripture and the guide provided with this session to explain to boys and girls how to become a Christian. Assign individuals to meet with kids who have more questions. If this is not possible, encourage boys and girls to ask their parents, small group leaders, and other Christian adults any questions they may have about becoming a Christian.

- **God rules.** God created and is in charge of everything. (Gen. 1:1; Rev. 4:11; Col. 1:16-17)
- **We sinned.** Since Adam and Eve, everyone has chosen to disobey God. (Rom. 3:23; 6:23)

- **God provided.** God sent His Son Jesus to rescue us from the punishment we deserve. (John 3:16; Eph. 2:8-9)
- **Jesus gives.** Jesus lived a perfect life, died on the cross for our sins, and rose again so we can be welcomed into God's family. (Rom. 5:8; 2 Cor. 5:21; 1 Pet. 3:18)
- **We respond.** Believe that Jesus alone saves you. Repent. Tell God that your faith is in Jesus. (Rom. 10:9-10,13)

Prayer (4 minutes)

- Big Picture Question Slide or Poster (enhanced CD)

Show the big picture question slide or poster.

Leader • Let's take one more look at our big picture question. *Why did God give His people the Ten Commandments? God is holy and wants His people to be holy.*

Encourage the kids to say the big picture question and answer all together 10 times. Invite them to hold up 10 fingers and then countdown together.

Before transitioning to small group, make any necessary announcements. Lead the kids in prayer. Thank God for giving us Jesus to come to God for us, and pray that kids will seek forgiveness through Jesus when they sin.

Dismiss to small groups

Small Group LEADER

Session Title: God Gave the Ten Commandments
Bible Passage: Exodus 19:1–20:21; 31:18; 32:1-35; 34:1-9
Big Picture Question: Why did God give His people the Ten Commandments? God is holy and wants His people to be holy.
Key Passage: Exodus 20:1-17
Unit Christ Connection: God instructed His covenant people how to live holy lives in an unholy world. This sustained their relationship with God until the perfect plan was revealed through Jesus Christ.

Key passage activity (5 minutes)

- Key Passage Slides or posters (enhanced CD)
- dry erase board and markers (optional)

Make sure the key passage, Exodus 20:1-17, is visible for each child, either as the printed posters or written on a dry erase board. Read the passage together.

Say • God was trying to teach His people how they could have a right relationship with Him. *Why did God give His people the Ten Commandments? God is holy and wants His people to be holy.* The problem is they were unable to live up to God's standard because of sin. We can't live up to God's standard either, but those who trust in Jesus are forgiven of their sins.

Repeat the key passage as a group several times. Read one of the commandments and ask the kids to identify what number it is. Repeat as time allows.

Bible story review (10 minutes)

- Bibles, 1 per kid
- Small Group Visual Pack
- Big Picture Question Slide or Poster (enhanced CD)
- tape
- marker
- CD player (optional)

Encourage the kids to find Exodus 19 in their Bibles. Help them as needed.

Say • The word *exodus* means going out or exiting. In which chapter in Exodus do we find all of the Ten Commandments? (*20*) Which division of the Bible is Exodus in? (*Law*) Exodus tells us how God used

Moses to rescue His people from Egypt and what God expected from His people.

Use the small group visual pack to show kids where today's Bible story is on the timeline. Review the Bible story provided or summarize the story in your own words. Place 10 small pieces of tape on the floor in a circle. Number them 1 to 10. Invite each kid to stand on one piece of tape. If you have more kids than spots, team kids up together. Play music or give the kids a command to walk. After a few minutes, stop the music or say "stop." Call out a number and ask the kid or kids on that number if they can tell you that commandment. Repeat until finished or as time allows.

Say • Do you think you could always keep the Ten Commandments? We all have broken some of these rules. If you ever wanted another kid's toy or took something that did not belong to you, you have sinned, too.

Show the big picture question slide or poster.

Say • That brings us to our big picture question. *Why did God give His people the Ten Commandments? God is holy and wants His people to be holy.* Because we sin, the only way we can be holy is through Jesus. He lived on earth without breaking a single command.

Activity choice (10 minutes)

Option 1: Hopscotch commandments

Use tape to make 10 squares in any pattern that you choose of one or two boxes. Make sure they are all connected. For example, you could tape one long line with one square box only or you could also create a common hopscotch pattern. Instruct the kids to line up single file in front of all the boxes. Give the first kid a small rock. The kid will toss the rock to make it land in one of the boxes. He will then jump

• tape
• small rock or beanbag

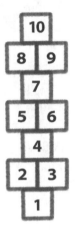

- paper, 1 per kid
- scissors, 1 per kid
- Key Passage Posters (enhanced CD)
- crayons or markers

to the item, pick it up, and jump back. Allow everyone to play. Repeat, asking the kids to throw the rock.

Option: When the kid reaches the square with the rock, he must recite that commandment before picking up the rock.

Advanced option: Count the blocks and invite the kids to say that number commandment as the current player jumps.

Say • God gave the Israelites the Ten Commandments. ***Why did God give His people the Ten Commandments? God is holy and wants His people to be holy.***

Option 2: Commandment hands

Distribute a piece of paper to each kid. Demonstrate how to fold the paper in half widthwise. Instruct each kid to place the paper in front of her with the fold to her left. She will place her left hand on the paper with her pinkie lined up with the fold and her wrist against the bottom of the paper. She must keep her pinkie straight, but stretch out her other fingers. Trace from the bottom of the paper near her thumb around each finger until going straight over the pinkie to the fold. Invite each kid to cut out the hand print. (It should open like a card with the two pinkies attached.) Cut the space between the two pinkies to where the pinkies meet the palm, revealing all 10 fingers, but do not cut the card apart. Using the key passage posters, encourage the kids to write the Ten Commandments on the inside of their card. Decorate the hands with crayons or markers.

Say • God gave the Israelites the Ten Commandments. The Israelites were supposed to remember and obey the commandments. ***Why did God give His people the Ten Commandments? God is holy and wants His people to be holy.***

- folder, 1 per kid
- Journal Page, 1 per kid (enhanced CD)
- markers or crayons
- Bible Story Coloring Page

Journal and prayer (5 minutes)

Distribute each child's journal and the journal page provided with this session. Instruct the kids to draw a mountain with a cloud over it that symbolizes God. Older kids can share what commandment they think is the hardest to keep.

Say • Who knows our big picture question and answer? *Why did God give His people the Ten Commandments? God is holy and wants His people to be holy.*

Make sure each child puts this week's sheet in his journal and then collect them. Keep the journals in the classroom so they will be available every week or as often as you wish to use them.

If time remains, take prayer requests or allow kids to color the coloring page provided with this session. End the session with prayer, thanking God for loving us so much. Pray for each child by name, and ask God to help her see how God is holy and sees us as holy only when we know and love Jesus.

Teacher BIBLE STUDY

Thirteen of the last sixteen chapters of the Book of Exodus consist of instructions for building the tabernacle. The word *tabernacle* means "dwelling place." The tabernacle was a portable tent where God met with His people. God had a great purpose for the tabernacle. (See Ex. 29:45-46.)

Moses had been on the mountain talking with God for 40 days. During that time, God wrote the Ten Commandments, the words of the covenant, on tablets. Moses called all of the Israelite community together and gave them the instructions God had given him. (Ex. 24:3-4)

God's directions for building the tabernacle were very detailed. God was not trying to burden the people; He was trying to show them His holiness and absolute authority. God appointed Bezalel and Oholiab to oversee the building of the tabernacle, giving them wisdom, understanding, and craftsmanship. Every skilled person "whose heart moved him" eagerly worked on the tabernacle of the Lord. (See Ex. 35:30-35; 36:1-6.)

God gave the Israelites the tabernacle as a visual picture of His dwelling with them. The tabernacle was a temporary place for God's glory to dwell until the coming of Christ. (2 Cor. 4:6) Every part of the tabernacle was designed to illustrate God's relationship with His people.

Christ is the New Testament fulfillment of the Old Testament tabernacle. John 1:14 says that "the Word became flesh and took up residence among us." Jesus made His dwelling with men. He tabernacled with them. (Rev. 21:3)

As you teach kids about the building of the tabernacle, show them God's desire to be with His people. Emphasize that Jesus was God's plan to bring people back to Himself.

Younger Kids BIBLE STUDY OVERVIEW

Session Title: The Tabernacle Was Built
Bible Passage: Exodus 35:4–40:38
Big Picture Question: What does the tabernacle show about God? God wants to dwell with His people and be worshiped by them.
Key Passage: Exodus 20:1-17
Unit Christ Connection: God instructed His covenant people how to live holy lives in an unholy world. This sustained their relationship with God until the perfect plan was revealed through Jesus Christ.

Small Group Opening

Large Group Leader

Small Group Leader

The BIBLE STORY

The Tabernacle Was Built
Exodus 35:4–40:38

When Moses was on the mountain talking to God, God said, "Tell the Israelites to make a sanctuary for Me so that I may dwell among them." God gave Moses very specific instructions for building the tabernacle and everything that went inside it. "Make it exactly like I show you," God said.

So when Moses went down the mountain, he gathered the entire Israelite community together. He told them everything God had said. He asked them to bring materials: gold, silver, and bronze; blue, purple, and scarlet yarn; fine linen and goat hair; animals skins; wood; oil; spices; and gemstones.

Moses called for anyone who was a skilled craftsman to make everything the Lord had commanded. This included the tabernacle and all its pieces, the ark of the covenant, the table for the bread of the Presence, the golden lampstand, and many other parts.

Every Israelite who felt moved in his heart brought an offering for the tabernacle. People came with gold jewelry; blue, purple, and scarlet yarn; fine linen and goat hair; animal skins; wood; oil; spices; and gemstones.

God gave two men, Bezalel (BEHZ uh lehl) and Oholiab (oh HOH lih ab), special skills for building and creating things. Bezalel, Oholiab, and all the skilled people came together to build the tabernacle for God. At the same time, people kept bringing offerings of what they had. Pretty soon, the craftsmen came to Moses and said, "The people are bringing more than enough. We don't need all of this to build the tabernacle as God instructed." So Moses told the Israelites to stop bringing their offerings.

Everyone who came together to build the tabernacle built it just as God had instructed Moses. There were 10 curtains made out of linen that were 42 feet long. Eleven curtains made out of goat hair formed a tent over the tabernacle. The planks of acacia wood were 15 feet long and 27 inches wide. Everything was done exactly as God had said.

Inside the tabernacle, the people made a veil. They made an ark, a table, a lampstand, and many other parts. Every part had its special purpose and was made just as God had said.

When the time had come, God told Moses how to erect the tabernacle. God told him how to anoint the tabernacle so that it would be holy. God told Moses to bring Aaron and his sons to the entrance of the tabernacle. Aaron put on the holy garments and Moses anointed him to be priest. Aaron's sons were also anointed so that they would serve God as priests too.

Moses did exactly what God commanded, and the tabernacle was finished. The cloud where God was covered the tabernacle, and God's glory filled the tabernacle. God made a sign for the people: if the cloud covered the tabernacle, the people would stay where they were. When the cloud lifted from the tabernacle, the Israelites would move and take the tabernacle with them. The cloud of the LORD was on the tabernacle during the day, and fire was inside the cloud at night. Every one of the Israelites could see it as they traveled.

Christ Connection: God instructed the Israelites to build a tabernacle so that He could dwell with them. God desires to be with His people. As part of His plan of salvation, God sent Jesus to "tabernacle," or dwell with people on earth.

Small Group OPENING

Session Title: The Tabernacle Was Built
Bible Passage: Exodus 35:4–40:38
Big Picture Question: What does the tabernacle show about God? God wants to dwell with His people and be worshiped by them.
Key Passage: Exodus 20:1-17
Unit Christ Connection: God instructed His covenant people how to live holy lives in an unholy world. This sustained their relationship with God until the perfect plan was revealed through Jesus Christ.

Welcome time

- building materials: blocks, craft sticks, chenille stems, interlocking bricks, and so on

Arriving Activity: Creative building

Provide some type of materials to build with (interlocking bricks, blocks, craft sticks, chenille stems, or anything else). As kids arrive, direct them to the building materials, and ask them to build something. They can build whatever they would like. Before class begins, allow them to talk about what they built.

Say • You took what you had and made something. Today we will talk about how God's people did the same thing. They were told to use what they had to build something very special.

Activity page (5 minutes)

- "What's Missing?" activity page, 1 per kid
- pencils

Guide boys and girls to complete the activity page.

Say • In a few moments, we are going to learn about the tabernacle. We will find out what was in it and why the Israelites built it.

Session starter (10 minutes)

Option 1: All together

Group kids in teams of two or four. Tape a start line and

- tape

finish line for each group. Lead each team to the start line. Each team member will stand directly in front of another team member. Groups of two should face each other and reach their arms straight out, locking their fingers together. Groups of four should lock the fingers of one hand with the team member across from them and lock the fingers of the other hand with the team member diagonal to them. When you say go, the teams will race one another to the finish line. If anyone lets go of a team member's hand at any point, the team must start over. Give the signal to go. Repeat as time allows.

Say • You had to work together to complete the race. God's people were also going to work together in today's Bible story to complete an important task.

Option 2: Offering envelopes

• envelope, 1 per kid
• crayons or markers
• stickers (optional)

Tip: You could use this craft as an opportunity to raise money for a special cause or event.

Provide an envelope for each child. Explain to the kids that they will make an offering envelope. Describe how their parents may use an envelope each week to give money to the church and how that money allows the church to have ministers, electricity, heat and air, and even classrooms like the one they are in. Provide markers or crayons to decorate. Use stickers or other decorations that you have available. Encourage the kids to bring the envelope back next week with their own offering in it.

Say • God's people gave offerings to build a special place for God. We will find out about that place in today's Bible story.

Transition to large group

Large Group LEADER

Session Title: The Tabernacle Was Built
Bible Passage: Exodus 35:4–40:38
Big Picture Question: What does the tabernacle show about God? God wants to dwell with His people and be worshiped by them.
Key Passage: Exodus 20:1-17
Unit Christ Connection: God instructed His covenant people how to live holy lives in an unholy world. This sustained their relationship with God until the perfect plan was revealed through Jesus Christ.

• countdown video

Countdown

Show the countdown video as your kids arrive, and set it to end as large group time begins.

• yarn

Introduce the session (1 minute)

[Large group leader enters with a roll of yarn.]

Leader • What do you think I could do with this yarn? Maybe I could make a scarf, but what if each of you had some yarn, too? We could make a few sweaters. Now, I want you to imagine. Last week, we learned God's people received the Ten Commandments. Now what? They were traveling through the wilderness. Does anyone know what the wilderness was? It sounds like a vast forest filled with tropical plants and all kinds of cuddly animals, right? Try again. The wilderness was a desert—mostly rocks, sand, and the kind of animals you don't want to meet. That's why God sent manna to the people and made rocks produce water.

• Timeline Map

Timeline map (1 minute)

Leader • Let's take a look at our timeline map to see where God took His people next. Remember, He was trying to get them to the promised land. That's the place where God told Abraham his family would one day be as numerous as the stars in the sky. Here it is. It says, "The Tabernacle Was Built." What is the tabernacle? It's a special place for God to be with His people.

Big picture question (1 minute)

• Big Picture Question Poster or Slide (enhanced CD)

Leader • You and I have a special place where we can find God. If you are a Christian, God not only dwells with you. He dwells in you. Because of what Jesus did on the cross, the Holy Spirit lives in you. The Holy Spirit guides you and directs you. Do you know how He guides and directs you? It's through God's Word. Speaking of God's Word, it's time for our Bible check. Let's see those Bibles. Great!

Let's get ready to use those Bibles, but before we get into our lesson, here is our big picture question: ***What does the tabernacle show about God?***

• "Give You Glory" song

Sing (5 minutes)

Leader • You may remember from last week that God gave the Ten Commandments to His people, but the people were scared of all the thunder and smoke and of God Himself. They asked Moses to meet with God and let Moses talk to them. Moses did that and he met with God on a mountain away from the people. Think about it. These people got to meet with the Creator of everything, and they asked Him to stay away. They saw just how awesome God was and were afraid it might kill them to be that close to Him. Aren't you glad that we can go to God because of what Jesus did for us? We can give God glory right here in this room.

Sing together "Give You Glory."

The Wilderness

Key passage (4 minutes)

• "Ten Commandments" song
• Key Passage Slides or Posters (enhanced CD)

Leader • How many of you remember one of the Ten Commandments? Let's see how well you remember them as we take a look at our key passage.

Show the slides or posters of this unit's key passage, Exodus 20:1-17. Lead the boys and girls to read the key passage together.

Leader • The first four commandments are all about God. The Israelites were told to only worship God, to not put other things before Him, to be respectful with His name, and to give Him one day of the week to honor Him. That's what we do on Sundays; we meet together here at church to honor Him. Let's honor Him right now by singing about His commandments.

Sing together "Ten Commandments."

Tell the Bible story (10 minutes)

• "The Tabernacle Was Built" video
• Bibles, 1 per kid
• Bible Story Picture Slide or Poster (enhanced CD)
• yarn

Leader • We talked earlier about how little I could do with this yarn, but if we all had yarn, we could do a lot. We are about to find out how God's people, though in the desert with few supplies, built the tabernacle by everyone giving a little. We will also answer our big picture question. *What does the tabernacle show about God?*

Open your Bible to Exodus 35. Choose to tell the Bible story in your own words using the script provided, or show the "The Tabernacle Was Built" video.

Leader • God asked Moses to tell the people to build a place where He could stay with them, a place they could take as they traveled. God wanted to be with His people and give them a place to worship Him. *What does the tabernacle show about God? God wants to dwell with His people and be worshiped by them.* Of course, the people didn't have a building supply store to visit. They were in the desert, but they did have all that stuff the Egyptians gave them before they left. Each Israelite gave as much as they wanted, and it turned out to be more than they needed. The tabernacle was a large tent with some very important items inside, each with a very special meaning. God also gave two men special gifts, so they could lead the people in building the tabernacle and all the things inside it. Moses then anointed Aaron and his sons to take care of the tabernacle as priests. When it was all done, it was exactly what God asked for. The cloud that symbolized God's presence came down and God's glory entered the tabernacle. Whenever the cloud moved, the people knew it was time for them to move, too.

Ask the following review questions:

1. How did God tell Moses to get the supplies to build the tabernacle? (*He asked the people to bring the things needed; Exodus 35:4-9,21*)

2. Who built the tabernacle? (*Bezalel, Oholiab, and other skilled workers from the people; Exodus 36:1*)

3. How did the people know God had entered the tabernacle? (*a cloud covered it, Exodus 40:34*)

4. How did the people know it was time to leave where they were staying? (*the cloud would leave the tabernacle, Exodus 40:37*)

5. Do we need a tabernacle to meet with God? (*No, God sent Jesus to "tabernacle" or dwell with people on earth.*)

Discussion starter video (4 minutes)

• "Worship Whom?" video

Leader • Do you want to dwell or be with God and worship Him? Have you put Him first? Sometimes we say we do but don't always show it, like in this video.

Play "Worship Whom?"

Leader • Have you ever acted that way? Do you like to go to church as much as going to the park or playing video games? Don't get me wrong: the church is very different from the tabernacle. For instance, we don't need a building to worship God. God dwells or stays in the hearts of His people. Because of sin, we could not go to God, so He came to us. Jesus came, lived a holy life, and died so we could once again be with God.

The Gospel: God's Plan for Me (optional)

Use Scripture and the guide provided with this session to explain to boys and girls how to become a Christian. Assign individuals to meet with kids who have more questions. If this is not possible, encourage boys and girls to ask their parents, small group leaders, and other Christian adults any questions they may have about becoming a Christian.

Prayer (4 minutes)

• Big Picture Question Slide or Poster (enhanced CD)

Show the big picture question slide or poster.

Leader • It's time for the answer to our big picture question. *What does the tabernacle show about God? God wants to dwell with His people and be worshiped by them.*

Ask the kids what they like better about coming to church, the music or the Bible story? Those that choose the music ask the big picture question, and those that choose the Bible story answer. Swap roles and repeat.

Before transitioning to small group, make any necessary announcements. Lead the kids in prayer. Thank God for wanting to be with us, and pray that the kids will want to be with Him, too.

The Gospel: God's Plan for Me

Ask kids if they have ever heard the word *gospel*. Clarify that the word *gospel* means "good news." It is the message about Christ, the kingdom of God, and salvation. Use the following guide to share the gospel with kids.

God rules. Explain to kids that the Bible tells us God created everything, and He is in charge of everything. Invite a volunteer to read Genesis 1:1 from the Bible. Read Revelation 4:11 or Colossians 1:16-17 aloud and explain what these verses mean.

We sinned. Tell kids that since the time of Adam and Eve, everyone has chosen to disobey God (Romans 3:23). The Bible calls this sin. Because God is holy, God cannot be around sin. Sin separates us from God and deserves God's punishment of death (Romans 6:23).

God provided. Choose a child to read John 3:16 aloud. Say that God sent His Son Jesus, the perfect solution to our sin problem, to rescue us from the punishment we deserve. It's something we, as sinners, could never earn on our own. Jesus alone saves us. Read and explain Ephesians 2:8-9.

Jesus gives. Share with kids that Jesus lived a perfect life, died on the cross for our sins, and rose again. Because Jesus gave up His life for us, we can be welcomed into God's family for eternity. This is the best gift ever! Read Romans 5:8, 2 Corinthians 5:21, or 1 Peter 3:18.

We respond. Tell kids that they can respond to Jesus. Read Romans 10:9-10,13. Review these aspects of our response: Believe in your heart that Jesus alone saves you through what He's already done on the cross. Repent, turning from self and sin to Jesus. Tell God and others that your faith is in Jesus.

Offer to talk with any child who is interested in responding to Jesus.

Small Group LEADER

Session Title: The Tabernacle Was Built
Bible Passage: Exodus 35:4–40:38
Big Picture Question: What does the tabernacle show about God? God wants to dwell with His people and be worshiped by them.
Key Passage: Exodus 20:1-17
Unit Christ Connection: God instructed His covenant people how to live holy lives in an unholy world. This sustained their relationship with God until the perfect plan was revealed through Jesus Christ.

- Key Passage Slides or Posters (enhanced CD)
- dry erase board and markers (optional)
- strip of paper

Key passage activity (5 minutes)

Make sure the key passage, Exodus 20:1-17, is visible for each child, either as the printed posters or written on a dry erase board. Read the passage together.

Say • God is holy and gave the people the Ten Commandments so they would understand how to live as God's people. God also made it clear in the first four commandments that He wants to be with His people. That's why He instructed them to build the tabernacle. *What does the tabernacle show about God? God wants to dwell with His people and be worshiped by them.*

Use a strip of paper to hide one of the commandments on the poster or dry erase board. See if the kids can tell you which one is missing. Repeat with each commandment.

Bible story review (10 minutes)

- Bibles, 1 per kid
- Small Group Visual Pack
- Big Picture Question Slide or Poster (enhanced CD)

Encourage the kids to find Exodus 35 in their Bibles. Help them as needed.

Say • What does *exodus* mean? (*going out or exiting*) In which chapter in Exodus do we find all the Ten Commandments? (*20*) Which division of the Bible

Younger Kids Bible Study Leader Guide
Unit 6 • Session 2

is Exodus in? (*Law*) What three major events have we seen in Exodus? (*Israelites freed from Egypt, the Ten Commandments, the building of the tabernacle*) Exodus tells us how God used Moses to rescue His people from Egypt, what God expected from His people, and how God would dwell or stay with His people.

Use the small group visual pack to show kids where today's Bible story is on the timeline. Review the Bible story provided or summarize the story in your own words.

Assign kids parts of the tabernacle before reviewing the story. Start by making four kids the tabernacle. Instruct them to come to the front when you first say "tabernacle." When they come forward, use them as corners to form a large square. Make sure each kid is a part of the tabernacle. If you just have a few kids, give only the key pieces. Kids can be the ark, the table, the lampstand, the curtains, or the veil. If you have several kids, assign them the parts of what the people brought. Encourage each kid to come stand inside the "human" tabernacle when you say the part assigned to him.

Say • How many of you are glad we don't need a building to come to God? We meet at church because the Bible tells us Christians should worship and serve together, but when you know and love Jesus, you don't need a building to be with God. Hebrews 9:11 says Jesus came into the perfect tabernacle for us so we can dwell with God through His Spirit.

Show the big picture question slide or poster.

Say • What a perfect reminder of our big picture question and answer! *What does the tabernacle show about God? God wants to dwell with His people and be worshiped by them.*

Activity choice (10 minutes)

Option 1: Church tour

Spend a few minutes talking about the different parts of the tabernacle. Explain that the tabernacle and the church have very little in common. Make sure they understand that the church is not God's dwelling place, but the place they come to worship with others. However, the church has some special parts. Take a few minutes to talk about the sanctuary, the altar, the baptistry, or any other special place in your church. If possible, take the kids on a tour of the church to show them some of these things.

Say • Just like the tabernacle, the church has some very special parts, too. *What does the tabernacle show about God? God wants to dwell with His people and be worshiped by them.*

Option 2: Tabernacle snack

- graham cracker, 1 per kid
- jumbo marshmallows, 4 per kid
- candy pieces
- "Tabernacle Picture" poster (enhanced CD)

Provide a graham cracker, four jumbo marshmallows, and some candy pieces. Tell the kids to make four corners with the marshmallows. The graham cracker will sit on top to form the tent. Before placing the graham cracker on top, use the picture of the tabernacle to explain the different parts inside the tabernacle. Invite the kids to place a candy piece where each item would be.

Say • The tabernacle was the place God dwelled or stayed with His people, the Israelites. Today, God dwells within those who trust in Jesus. *What does the tabernacle show about God? God wants to dwell with His people and be worshiped by them.*

- folder, 1 per kid
- Journal Page, 1 per kid (enhanced CD)
- markers or crayons
- Bible Story Coloring Page

Journal and Prayer (5 minutes)

Distribute each child's journal and the journal page provided with this session. Instruct the kids to draw their own picture of the tabernacle. Older kids can try to name some of the parts.

Say • Here's one last look at our big picture question and answer. *What does the tabernacle show about God? God wants to dwell with His people and be worshiped by them.*

Make sure each child puts this week's sheet in his journal and then collect them. Keep the journals in the classroom so they will be available every week or as often as you wish to use them.

If time remains, take prayer requests or allow kids to color the coloring page provided with this session. End the session with prayer, thanking God for using the tabernacle to show us how He wants to be with us. Pray for each child by name, and ask God to help him spend time with God this week in prayer and Bible study.

Teacher BIBLE STUDY

The tabernacle was complete. God now had a place where His glory could dwell without causing the Israelites to fear death. God had given His people laws from the mountain, and He gave them more rules for living and worshiping Him when He dwelled in the tabernacle. These rules are recorded in the Book of Leviticus. The reasoning behind Leviticus can be found in Leviticus 19:2.

In Leviticus 17:11, God set apart the blood of a creature as the means for making atonement. This answers the question, "Why did Jesus have to die?" God's requirement for the forgiveness of sins was the shedding of blood: "According to the law almost everything is purified with blood, and without the shedding of blood there is no forgiveness" (Heb. 9:22).

It is important to note a New Testament revelation about the sin offering. Hebrews 10:4 says, "It is impossible for the blood of bulls and goats to take away sins." Then why did God require people to make sacrifices? The institution of a sacrifice was to point to something greater—the ultimate sacrifice God would make by sending His own Son, Jesus Christ, to pay for the sins of the world once and for all. (See Eph. 1:7; Rom 5:9.) The Book of Leviticus contains many rules for the Israelite people, but we do not obey all the rules in Leviticus today because we trust Jesus, who obeyed the law perfectly for us.

Many of the kids you teach will not be familiar with the Book of Leviticus. Use this session as an opportunity to emphasize God's holiness and His requirement of a blood sacrifice for the forgiveness of sins. Lead them to treasure Jesus as the perfect and final sacrifice that took away the sin of the world. (John 1:29)

Younger Kids BIBLE STUDY OVERVIEW

Session Title: God Gave Rules for Sacrifice

Bible Passage: Leviticus 1–27

Big Picture Question: Why did God require a blood sacrifice? Because God is holy, His forgiveness requires a payment for sin. Jesus made the ultimate payment for sin with His death on the cross.

Key Passage: Exodus 20:1-17

Unit Christ Connection: God instructed His covenant people how to live holy lives in an unholy world. This sustained their relationship with God until the perfect plan was revealed through Jesus Christ.

Small Group Opening

Large Group Leader

Small Group Leader

The BIBLE STORY

God Gave Rules for Sacrifice
Leviticus 1–27

When Moses was with God on Mount Sinai, God gave him many rules and laws that the Israelites were to obey. God required the people to obey His law perfectly because God is holy. He cannot be around sin. He wants His people to be holy. Now that the tabernacle was built, Moses didn't have to go up the mountain anymore. He could go into the tabernacle to meet with God. From the tabernacle, God gave Moses more laws. These laws told the people of Israel how to worship God and how to live holy lives.

First, God gave rules about offerings. Offerings are gifts people give to God, such as money or jewelry. Sometimes offerings included animals. Grain and bread could also be given as offerings. Different types of offerings were needed at different times. When people wanted to praise God, they gave burnt offerings. When they wanted to say they were sorry for sin, they gave a sin offering.

God also gave rules about the priests. Priests made the sacrifices that God commanded. The priests took care of the tabernacle, and they taught the people God's rules for living holy lives. Aaron and his sons served as the priests. God gave them rules about how to offer sacrifices.

God told Moses about a special day that would happen once a year. It was called the Day of Atonement. *Atonement* means making right what had been wrong. The people needed to atone for their sin to make their relationship with God right again. On the Day of Atonement, the people paid for their sins. On that day, the high priest offered a special sacrifice. He took the blood of an animal and went into the most holy place, a very special room in the tabernacle. Then the high priest sprinkled the blood on the mercy seat of the ark of the covenant, which was a wooden box covered in gold that contained the stone tablets on which the Ten Commandments were written.

The sacrifice was important because it paid for the sins of the people of Israel. God said, "On that day your sin will be paid for. You will be made pure and clean. You will be clean from all of your sins in my sight."

God also gave the Israelites rules about how they should live. He said, "Be holy because I, Yahweh your God, am holy." God told the people how to be holy. God said, "Do not tell lies. Do not cheat. Love your neighbor as you love yourself. Obey my rules."

Christ Connection: The Book of Leviticus contains many rules for the Israelites, but we do not obey all the rules in Leviticus today because we trust Jesus, who obeyed the law perfectly for us. The Israelites had to make a blood sacrifice for their sin every year. Jesus sacrificed His blood on the cross to pay for our sin once and for all. (Hebrews 7:26-27) When we trust in Christ, God forgives us of our sin.

Small Group OPENING

Session Title: God Gave Rules for Sacrifice
Bible Passage: Leviticus 1–27
Big Picture Question: Why did God require a blood sacrifice? Because God is holy, His forgiveness requires a payment for sin. Jesus made the ultimate payment for sin with His death on the cross.
Key Passage: Exodus 20:1-17
Unit Christ Connection: God instructed His covenant people how to live holy lives in an unholy world. This sustained their relationship with God until the perfect plan was revealed through Jesus Christ.

Welcome time

Arriving Activity: In trouble

Talk about what happens when you do something wrong. Share a time you were a kid and got in trouble. What punishment did you get? Allow the kids to share something they got in trouble for, too.

Say • Did you each deserve the punishment you got? We deserve punishment when we do something wrong. God's people, the Israelites, sinned against God just like you and me. They deserved punishment. Jesus had not come yet as their sacrifice. The good news is God had a temporary plan for them. We'll find out more in today's Bible story.

Activity page (5 minutes)

• "Gifts to God" activity page, 1 per kid
• pencils

Guide boys and girls to complete the activity page.

Say • Money, jewelry, animals, and grain were all types of offerings the people were told to give to God. In a few moments, we will find out why.

Session starter (10 minutes)

Option 1: Penny toss

• penny, 1 per kid
• paper plate

Provide each child with a penny or other coin. Guide the kids to form a circle and place a paper plate in the middle. When you give the command to go, kids toss their penny. The winner will be the first child to toss her penny into the "offering" plate. Invite the kids to retrieve their penny, and play again. Continue as time allows.

Say • Money is an offering we give to God today, but it's an offering that people have been giving to God for thousands of years. You'll find out more in today's Bible story.

Option 2: Pay up

• grocery items
• index cards,
  1 per grocery item

Bring in some grocery items. Write the price for each item on an index card. Choose a volunteer to come up and guess how much one of the items costs. Invite the other kids to share what they think the price is with the volunteer, but the volunteer gets the final guess. Reveal the price of the item. Repeat with another volunteer.

Say • Everything has a price, including sin. Today, we will find out what that price of sin was for the Israelites.

Transition to large group

Large Group LEADER

Session Title: God Gave Rules for Sacrifice
Bible Passage: Leviticus 1–27
Big Picture Question: Why did God require a blood sacrifice? Because God is holy, His forgiveness requires a payment for sin. Jesus made the ultimate payment for sin with His death on the cross.
Key Passage: Exodus 20:1-17
Unit Christ Connection: God instructed His covenant people how to live holy lives in an unholy world. This sustained their relationship with God until the perfect plan was revealed through Jesus Christ.

Countdown

• countdown video

Show the countdown video as your kids arrive, and set it to end as large group time begins.

Introduce the session (1 minute)

• loaf of bread

[Large group leader enters with a loaf of bread.]
Leader • How many of you like bread? Maybe you like to eat it as part of a sandwich or the bottom part of a pizza. Have you ever thought of offering bread to God? That may sound odd to you, but it wouldn't if you were an Israelite. As a grain offering, bread was one of the options God gave His people for an offering to Him. In the wilderness, grain would have been of great value. It wouldn't have looked like this. It would have looked more like a thick cracker because it had to be unleavened, which means it would not puff up like the bread you are used to.

Timeline map (1 minute)

• Timeline Map

Leader • Let's look at our timeline. Let's see where we've been and where we are headed. God freed His people from the Egyptians. He gave His people rules or commandments to live by. Then He instructed them on how to build a tabernacle so He could be with them. Now, we find ourselves here: "God Gave Rules for Sacrifice."

Big picture question (1 minute)

Leader • A *sacrifice* is something brought to God to express obedience, love, thanksgiving, or the need for forgiveness. Did you know your Bible tells us of the greatest sacrifice ever? Jesus gave His life so we could be forgiven. If you have your Bible, let's see it. Awesome!

Are you ready for our big picture question then? *Why did God require a blood sacrifice?*

Sing (5 minutes)

• "Give You Glory" song

Leader • You see, the Israelites were unable to keep the Ten Commandments God gave them. They could not be holy like God. God could not remain with people who were sinful. They didn't have Jesus as their sacrifice yet. God knew that and had a plan. He would give them rules on how to sacrifice to Him as payment for their sin. Aren't you glad that when we trust in Jesus' sacrifice for our sin, we are free to know and love Him? Once you accept Jesus' sacrifice to pay for your sins, you are able to give God glory in how you live.

Sing together "Give You Glory."

Key passage (4 minutes)

• "Ten Commandments" song
• Key Passage Slides or Posters (enhanced CD)

Leader • It's time to see if you remember the Ten Commandments God gave His people.

Show the slides or posters of this unit's key passage, Exodus 20:1-17. Lead the boys and girls to read the key passage together.

Leader • The last six commandments were about how God's people must treat others. They must honor their parents. They must not kill, break their marriage promises, steal, lie about each other, and want other people's things. We all struggle with one or more of these rules. We can't live without sinning, but Jesus did. He lived perfectly and died to cover our sins. And now we have new hearts that want to follow the Ten Commandments. Let's sing them together.

Sing together "Ten Commandments."

Tell the Bible story (10 minutes)

• "God Gave Rules for Sacrifice" video
• Bibles, 1 per kid
• Bible Story Picture Slides or Posters (enhanced CD)

Leader • No matter how hard they tried, the Israelites could not obey all of God's commandments all the time. Since God is holy, their sin had to be paid for, or God could not be with them. That brings us to our Bible story, and what a grain sacrifice is about. More importantly, we will answer our big picture question. *Why did God require a blood sacrifice?*

Open your Bible to Leviticus. Choose to tell the Bible story in your own words using the script provided, or show the "God Gave Rules for Sacrifice" video.

Leader • Moses met with God in the tabernacle, and God gave him more rules to explain to the people. These rules would explain how they should worship and how they could live holy lives. Many of these rules were about offerings or sacrifices. When the people wanted to praise God, they gave offerings of money, jewelry, grain and bread, and sometimes animals. Much of Leviticus is about how to give a sin offering. A sin offering required the blood of an animal. The Israelites made this sacrifice at least once a year on the Day of Atonement. This may be hard for us to understand, but the blood of the animals was a temporary solution for the Israelites because they didn't have Jesus, who gave His blood as a sacrifice for sin. ***Why did God require a blood sacrifice? Because God is holy, His forgiveness requires a payment for sin. Jesus made the ultimate payment for sin with His death on the cross.***

Ask the following review questions:

1. Where did God meet with Moses to give him rules about sacrifices? (*the tabernacle, Leviticus 1:1*)
2. Who did God choose to present the offerings? (*Aaron's sons or the priests, Leviticus 1:7-8*)
3. What was the Day of Atonement? (*The Israelites would give a sin offering on this day each year, Leviticus 16:29-30*)
4. God told the Israelites to live what kind of life? (*holy, Leviticus 19:2*)
5. Who is the perfect sacrifice who gave His blood for us? (*Jesus*)

Discussion starter video (4 minutes)

• "Not Enough" video

Leader • The Israelites had to make a payment for their sin. Often, things we need and want come with a price.

Play "Not Enough."

Leader • Have you ever wanted something so bad, but just didn't have the money for it? The payment for sin is something the Israelites couldn't pay either. No matter how hard they tried, they all sinned. The only payment for sin is blood. A perfect animal had to die to pay for their sins. The problem is that this wasn't enough. The life of even the most perfect animal wouldn't make the people holy. They needed a better substitute. That's why we have Jesus. The Israelites' imperfect sacrifice points us to the true, perfect sacrifice. In Matthew 26:28, Jesus told His

disciples at the Last Supper that His blood would cover the sins of many. There is no need to ever have another animal sacrifice. Jesus' blood is all that is needed.

The Gospel: God's Plan for Me (optional)

Use Scripture and the guide provided with this session to explain to boys and girls how to become a Christian. Assign individuals to meet with kids who have more questions. If this is not possible, encourage boys and girls to ask their parents, small group leaders, and other Christian adults any questions they may have about becoming a Christian.

Prayer (4 minutes)

• Big Picture Question Slide or Poster (enhanced CD)

Show the big picture question slide or poster.

Leader • Here's one more quick look at our big picture question. *Why did God require a blood sacrifice? Because God is holy, His forgiveness requires a payment for sin. Jesus made the ultimate payment for sin with His death on the cross.*

Divide the room into three sections. Ask the kids in the first section to ask the question. Invite the kids in the second section to give the first sentence of the answer and the third section to give the second sentence of the answer. Swap roles and repeat as time allows.

Before transitioning to small group, make any necessary announcements. Lead the kids in prayer. Thank God for giving us the perfect sacrifice in Jesus.

Dismiss to small groups

The Gospel: God's Plan for Me

Ask kids if they have ever heard the word *gospel*. Clarify that the word *gospel* means "good news." It is the message about Christ, the kingdom of God, and salvation. Use the following guide to share the gospel with kids.

God rules. Explain to kids that the Bible tells us God created everything, and He is in charge of everything. Invite a volunteer to read Genesis 1:1 from the Bible. Read Revelation 4:11 or Colossians 1:16-17 aloud and explain what these verses mean.

We sinned. Tell kids that since the time of Adam and Eve, everyone has chosen to disobey God (Romans 3:23). The Bible calls this sin. Because God is holy, God cannot be around sin. Sin separates us from God and deserves God's punishment of death (Romans 6:23).

God provided. Choose a child to read John 3:16 aloud. Say that God sent His Son Jesus, the perfect solution to our sin problem, to rescue us from the punishment we deserve. It's something we, as sinners, could never earn on our own. Jesus alone saves us. Read and explain Ephesians 2:8-9.

Jesus gives. Share with kids that Jesus lived a perfect life, died on the cross for our sins, and rose again. Because Jesus gave up His life for us, we can be welcomed into God's family for eternity. This is the best gift ever! Read Romans 5:8; 2 Corinthians 5:21; or 1 Peter 3:18.

We respond. Tell kids that they can respond to Jesus. Read Romans 10:9-10,13. Review these aspects of our response: Believe in your heart that Jesus alone saves you through what He's already done on the cross. Repent, turning from self and sin to Jesus. Tell God and others that your faith is in Jesus.

Offer to talk with any child who is interested in responding to Jesus.

Small Group LEADER

Session Title: God Gave Rules for Sacrifice
Bible Passage: Leviticus 1–27
Big Picture Question: Why did God require a blood sacrifice? Because God is holy, His forgiveness requires a payment for sin. Jesus made the ultimate payment for sin with His death on the cross.
Key Passage: Exodus 20:1-17
Unit Christ Connection: God instructed His covenant people how to live holy lives in an unholy world. This sustained their relationship with God until the perfect plan was revealed through Jesus Christ.

- Key Passage Slides or Posters (enhanced CD)
- dry erase board and markers (optional)

Key passage activity (5 minutes)

Make sure the key passage, Exodus 20:1-17, is visible for each child, either as the printed posters or written on a dry erase board. Read the passage together.

Say • If you do something wrong at your house, what happens? You get punished. The Israelites sinned against God. They couldn't keep the Ten Commandments. They deserved punishment. Since God can't be where sin is, their punishment would have been to be forever separated from God. Because God loved His people and promised to be their God, He provided animal sacrifices until Jesus came as the true sacrifice. *Why did God require a blood sacrifice? Because God is holy, His forgiveness requires a payment for sin. Jesus made the ultimate payment for sin with His death on the cross.* And now we are free to know and love God and obey His Ten Commandments.

Allow volunteers to share all the commandments they can remember. If a volunteer gets at least five right, encourage the kids to give her a "high five." If a volunteer gets all 10 correct, encourage the kids to all give him a "high 10." Feel free to give hints for kids to at least hit the "high five" mark.

Bible story review (10 minutes)

- Bibles, 1 per kid
- Small Group Visual Pack
- Big Picture Question Slides or Posters (enhanced CD)

Encourage the kids to find Leviticus in their Bibles. Help them as needed.

Say • Is Leviticus in the New Testament or Old Testament? (*Old Testament*) What does Leviticus tell us about? (*offerings and sacrifices*) Which division of the Bible is Leviticus in? (*Law*) What other books are in the Law division? (*Genesis, Exodus, Numbers, Deuteronomy*)

Use the small group visual pack to show kids where today's Bible story is on the timeline. Review the Bible story provided or summarize the story in your own words. Make sure kids understand that we don't give offerings or sacrifices like the Israelites did. Spend a few minutes talking about offerings we can give to God. Examples include: our time, our obedience, our money, our worship, our love.

Say • God does not need our offerings. However, when we know and love Jesus, we have a desire to give God our best in everything we do.

Show the big picture question slide or poster.

Say • Does anyone know the answer to our big picture question? ***Why did God require a blood sacrifice? Because God is holy, His forgiveness requires a payment for sin. Jesus made the ultimate payment for sin with His death on the cross.***

• "The Gospel: God's Plan for Me" poster (enhanced CD)

Activity choice (10 minutes)

Option 1: The plan

Display "The Gospel: God's Plan for Me" poster. Notice the icons beside each segment. Illustrate the following motions. For "God Rules," put both hands over the top of your head as if putting a crown on your head. For "We Sinned," make an *X* by crossing your arms. For "God Provided," rotate your crossed arms until you form a cross. For "Jesus Gives," put both hands and arms forward as if handing someone a box. For "We Respond," bring the hands back to your chest. Say the headers as you make the motions. Challenge the kids to go a little faster each time without messing up. Once finished, talk about what each header means.

Say • Because of the sacrifice Jesus made, we don't have to kill an animal. We just trust in Jesus' sacrifice. ***Why did God require a blood sacrifice? Because God is holy, His forgiveness requires a payment for sin. Jesus made the ultimate payment for sin with His death on the cross.***

Option 2: Paper clip necklace

• paper clips

Provide each kid with 25 to 30 colored paper clips or 20 to 25 large colored paper clips. Demonstrate how to hook the paper clips together to form a chain. Allow the kids to make necklaces. If you would like, hook the inside loop of a large paper clip with the inside loop of a small paper clip to form a cross. Hang the cross in the middle of the necklace.

Say • Jewelry was one of the offerings the Israelites gave to God. However, only a blood sacrifice was given as a sin offering. ***Why did God require a blood sacrifice? Because God is holy, His forgiveness requires a payment for sin. Jesus made the ultimate payment for sin with His death on the cross.***

Journal and Prayer (5 minutes)

- folder, 1 per kid
- Journal Page, 1 per kid (enhanced CD)
- markers or crayons
- Bible Story Coloring Page

Distribute each child's journal and the journal page provided with this session. Instruct the kids to draw a picture of a cross. Older kids can write the big picture question and answer.

Say • Let's all say the big picture question and answer together. *Why did God require a blood sacrifice? Because God is holy, His forgiveness requires a payment for sin. Jesus made the ultimate payment for sin with His death on the cross.*

Make sure each child puts this week's sheet in his journal and then collect them. Keep the journals in the classroom so they will be available every week or as often as you wish to use them.

If time remains, take prayer requests or allow kids to color the coloring page provided with this session. End the session with prayer, thanking God that Jesus was willing to give His life so we wouldn't have to give ours. Ask God to give the kids chances to offer their worship, time, obedience, money, and love this week.

Teacher BIBLE STUDY

Before God rescued His people from the Egyptians, He made a promise. God promised to bring the Israelites back to the land He had given to Abraham so many years ago. (Ex. 3:8)

God was leading the Israelites to the promised land. When they were close, God instructed Moses to send spies into the land to scout it out. The spies traveled around the land for 40 days, and it was just as God had promised. There was one problem; the people in the land were big and strong.

Caleb, one of the spies, announced, "We must go up and take possession of the land because we can certainly conquer it." Caleb understood that God was with them. With God's help, they could do anything. Joshua and Caleb understood who God is. When God promises to do something, He will do it. (Num. 23:19)

But the other men were afraid. That night all of the people wept loudly. They despaired because they did not believe God's promise to lead them into the promised land. The people plotted to find a new leader who would lead them back to Egypt.

God was not happy with Israel. They had turned away from Him and trusted in themselves. God wanted to destroy the people, but Moses interceded for them. God struck down the spies except for Caleb and Joshua, and He declared that anyone who had sinned against Him would not enter the promised land. The Israelites would wander in the desert for 40 more years.

Help the kids you teach understand that the Israelites sinned when they believed God was not in control. Point out that Joshua's obedience to God, which resulted in his leading the Israelites into the promised land, reminds us of Christ's life of obedience leading to His finished work on the cross, making the way into the promised land of eternity.

Younger Kids BIBLE STUDY OVERVIEW

Session Title: Joshua and Caleb
Bible Passage: Numbers 13:1–14:38
Big Picture Question: What happens when God's people sin? Sin has a price, but God forgives when people seek forgiveness.
Key Passage: Exodus 20:1-17
Unit Christ Connection: God instructed His covenant people how to live holy lives in an unholy world. This sustained their relationship with God until the perfect plan was revealed through Jesus Christ.

Small Group Opening

Large Group Leader

Small Group Leader

The BIBLE STORY

Joshua and Caleb
Numbers 13:1–14:38

God told Moses, "Send men to scout out the land of Canaan (KAY nuhn) I am giving to the Israelites." God instructed Moses to send out one leader from each family tribe. Moses sent them from the wilderness just as God commanded. All the men were leaders in Israel.

When Moses sent the men to scout out the land of Canaan, he told them, "Go up this way to the Negev (NEH gehv), then go up into the hill country. See what the land is like, and whether the people who live there are strong or weak, few or many." Moses had a lot of questions he wanted answered: Is the land good or bad? Are the cities they live in camps or forts? Is the land fertile or unproductive? Are there trees in it or not?

Moses said to the men, "Be courageous."

So the men went and scouted out the land. They traveled around the land for 40 days. When they were in the valley, they cut down a cluster of grapes and carried it on a pole. Then they went back to Moses, Aaron, and the Israelite community. They reported to Moses, "We went into the land where you sent us. Indeed, it is flowing with milk and honey. However, the people living in the land are strong, and the cities they live in are large and fortified. We saw groups of people living in the land and along the sea."

Caleb, one of the spies sent to scout out the land, said, "We must go up and take possession of the land! We can certainly conquer it with God's help!"

But the other men disagreed. "We can't go up against the people; they are stronger than we are! We look like grasshoppers compared to them!"

All of the Israelites started crying, and they cried all night. They thought Moses and Aaron had brought them to Canaan to die. They said, "Let's appoint a new leader and go back to Egypt!"

Moses and Aaron fell on their faces before all of the Israelites. Joshua and Caleb, who were among those who scouted out the land, tore their clothes and said to the Israelite community, "The land we passed through and explored is extremely good land. If the LORD is pleased with us, He will give it to us. Don't be afraid of the people living in the land; God is with us!"

"How long will these people despise Me?" God asked Moses. "How long will they not trust Me?" God wanted to destroy all the people, but Moses said, "Please pardon the wrongdoing of the people. I know You are great, faithful, and loving."

God replied, "Since you have asked, I will forgive them. But none of them who despised Me will live to see the promised land of Canaan." Since Caleb and Joshua had followed God completely, God decided to let them enter the promised land. God said that the people who did not trust that God would help them would face consequences for their sin for 40 years. They would wander in the wilderness and not enter the promised land. Out of all the spies who went to scout out the land, all of them died except for Joshua and Caleb.

Christ Connection: Even though Joshua was not perfect, he lived a life of obedience to God. Joshua was faithful and was going to lead the people into the promised land. His accomplishments point to Christ's finished work on the cross—defeating Satan, setting people free from sin, and making the way into the promised land of eternity.

Small Group OPENING

Session Title: Joshua and Caleb
Bible Passage: Numbers 13:1–14:38
Big Picture Question: What happens when God's people sin? Sin has a price, but God forgives when people seek forgiveness.
Key Passage: Exodus 20:1-17
Unit Christ Connection: God instructed His covenant people how to live holy lives in an unholy world. This sustained their relationship with God until the perfect plan was revealed through Jesus Christ.

Welcome time
Arriving Activity: I Spy

Play the game "I Spy" as kids arrive. Choose a volunteer who secretly looks for something in the room. The volunteer shares the color of that object by saying, "I spy something yellow." The other kids try to guess what object the volunteer is talking about. Whoever guesses the correct object is the next volunteer.

Say • In today's Bible story, a group of Israelites will be playing a real game of "I Spy."

- "Fruits Everywhere" activity page, 1 per kid
- pencils

Activity page (5 minutes)

Guide boys and girls to complete the activity page.

Say • God had a special place ready for His people to live that had lots of fruit to eat and plenty of land for each family. We'll find out what the Israelites said and did when they got there.

Session starter (10 minutes)

Option 1: Investigate game

Choose a volunteer and ask her to stand outside the room or face away from the class. The other kids then help choose an item in the room. The volunteer is invited to figure out what the object is. The rest of the kids cannot say anything. They only clap if the volunteer starts going toward the object. The closer the volunteer gets, the faster the kids should clap. When she identifies the object, the class responds by standing and clapping.

Say • God's people were looking for clues about a place that had been chosen for them to live. They had a choice to make based on what they found.

• paper plate or towel, 1 per kid
• variety of fruits

Tip: Consider food allergy issues when choosing snack items. Ask children or their parents for any allergy information, or post an allergy alert on the door where parents can see it.

Option 2: Fruit bowl

Provide each kid with a paper plate or paper towel. Let kids have a taste of some fruits. Try to provide grapes as part of the selection. Just a few pieces are all that's needed.

Say • How many of you would like to live in a place where you could have fruits anytime you wanted? That place existed for God's people, the Israelites. However, something stood in their way of taking it.

Transition to large group

Large Group LEADER

Session Title: Joshua and Caleb
Bible Passage: Numbers 13:1–14:38
Big Picture Question: What happens when God's people sin? Sin has a price, but God forgives when people seek forgiveness.
Key Passage: Exodus 20:1-17
Unit Christ Connection: God instructed His covenant people how to live holy lives in an unholy world. This sustained their relationship with God until the perfect plan was revealed through Jesus Christ.

• countdown video

Countdown

Show the countdown video as your kids arrive, and set it to end as large group time begins.

Introduce the session (1 minute)

• grapes

[Large group leader enters with a bunch of grapes.]
Leader • You wouldn't expect to find these in the desert, would you? Who would love to eat one of these grapes? Now, think about this. What if you had eaten the same thing every day for months? Now, imagine these grapes are one of the things you have not eaten. I bet they would look even better to you.

Timeline map (1 minute)

• Timeline Map

Leader • The Israelites were now free. God had given them rules, set up a place to be with them, and even given them a way to be forgiven when they didn't obey the rules He gave them. Long ago, God promised to bless Abraham, and God said that eventually his family would be a very large nation. He also promised the land Abraham was living on would be their land. God was making those promises happen. The Israelties were a nation of many people, but they were walking through the desert. Let's see where they are headed next. Here we go. Today's Bible story is "Joshua and Caleb."

Big picture question (1 minute)

Leader • We have only one place to find out more about Joshua and Caleb. Does anyone know where? Your Bible. Does anyone have your Bible with you today? Hold it up.

It's time for our big picture question. *What happens when God's people sin?*

Sing (5 minutes)

• "Give You Glory" song

Leader • Through offerings or sacrifices, God gave the Israelites a way to seek forgiveness. However, we also need to understand God's response or what He says and does when His people don't live a holy life. Our lives are meant to give God glory. We can only do that as we know and love Jesus and respond to that knowledge and love in a way that honors God. We want to give God glory. Let's sing to Him.

Sing together "Give You Glory."

Key passage (4 minutes)

• "Ten Commandments" song
• Key Passage Slides or Posters (enhanced CD)

Leader • In a few minutes we are going to learn about Joshua and Caleb and how they understood who God is when no one else did. They had paid attention to all those times when God provided. They believed His promises. They even desired to follow the rules God gave, what we call the Ten Commandments.

Show the slides or posters of this unit's key passage, Exodus 20:1-17. Lead the boys and girls to read the key passage together.

Leader • The Israelites had already disobeyed these

commands more than once. Moses had pleaded to God for them, and God forgave them. Let's see if we can remember the commands God gave them as we sing them together.

Sing together "Ten Commandments."

Tell the Bible story (10 minutes)

Leader • Now we come to the Bible story. The people, who had already disobeyed God several times, once again faced the opportunity to believe God and His promises or choose their own way over His. That's when we will be able to answer our big picture question. *What happens when God's people sin?*

Open your Bible to Numbers 13. Choose to tell the Bible story in your own words using the script provided, or show the "Joshua and Caleb" video.

Leader • God brought the people to the land He had promised them hundreds of years earlier, and He told Moses to send 12 spies to look at the land. He wanted to see what the land was like. They spent 40 days looking and came back with a single cluster of grapes that took two men to carry it. Can you imagine?

The spies told Moses the land would be a great place to live, but people were already living there. Caleb and Joshua spoke up and said that God would give them the land, but all the other spies saw was the people who lived there. They were scared of the people and said the Israelites would be like grasshoppers to them.

The people chose to side with those who gave the bad reports. Moses again asked God to forgive them. He did, but this time they had a big price to pay. *What happens when God's people sin? Sin has a price, but God forgives when people seek forgiveness.*

- "Joshua and Caleb" video
- Bibles, 1 per kid
- Bible Story Picture Slide or Poster (enhanced CD)

The price would be that the people who had sinned by refusing to believe God would never see the land He promised. They would instead spend 40 years in the wilderness. God told Moses that Joshua, Caleb, and the children would be the only ones who would one day live in the land. As a matter of fact, it was Joshua who eventually led the people into the promise land.

Ask the following review questions:

1. How many spies did God tell Moses to send into the land? (*12, Numbers 13:1-15*)

2. What did they say about the land? (*It was good land with lots of food but strong people living there, Numbers 13:27-28*)

3. Who said they should take the land? (*Joshua and Caleb, Numbers 13:30; 14:6-9*)

4. What was the punishment for the sin of those who did not trust God to give them the land? (*They would never live in the land they were promised, Numbers 14:22-23*)

5. Who leads us into the promised land of eternity when we put our trust in Him? (*Jesus*)

Discussion starter video (4 minutes)

• "Make Your Choice" video

Leader • Have you ever had to make a tough choice? Watch this video.

Play "Make Your Choice."

Leader • Have any of you ever had to make a choice that you didn't know how to make? Sometimes what seems like the easy choice is not always the right choice. It makes sense that the Israelites saw all those big people and decided that they should stay away. The problem was they knew God had led them there and that God had promised that land to them. After all they had seen God do, they still didn't trust Him. Joshua and Caleb were

different. They believed God would get them the land even though it looked impossible. Joshua eventually led the people into the land. He was not perfect, but in this case he was obedient and faithful to God. Jesus was obedient, faithful, and perfect. He will also lead His people—those who know and love Him—to a different promised land: a place called heaven.

The Gospel: God's Plan for Me (optional)

Use Scripture and the guide provided with this session to explain to boys and girls how to become a Christian. Assign individuals to meet with kids who have more questions. If this is not possible, encourage boys and girls to ask their parents, small group leaders, and other Christian adults any questions they may have about becoming a Christian.

Prayer (4 minutes)

• Big Picture Question Slide or Poster (enhanced CD)

Show the big picture question slide or poster.

Leader • Here's our big picture question and answer. *What happens when God's people sin? Sin has a price, but God forgives when people seek forgiveness.*

Choose two volunteers to play the roles of Joshua and Caleb. Encourage them to ask the big picture question. Instruct the remaining kids to give the answer. Choose two new volunteers and repeat as time allows.

Before transitioning to small group, make any necessary announcements. Lead the kids in prayer. Thank God for giving forgiveness, and pray that the kids will ask for forgiveness when they sin.

Dismiss to small groups

The Gospel: God's Plan for Me

Ask kids if they have ever heard the word *gospel*. Clarify that the word *gospel* means "good news." It is the message about Christ, the kingdom of God, and salvation. Use the following guide to share the gospel with kids.

God rules. Explain to kids that the Bible tells us God created everything, and He is in charge of everything. Invite a volunteer to read Genesis 1:1 from the Bible. Read Revelation 4:11 or Colossians 1:16-17 aloud and explain what these verses mean.

We sinned. Tell kids that since the time of Adam and Eve, everyone has chosen to disobey God (Romans 3:23). The Bible calls this sin. Because God is holy, God cannot be around sin. Sin separates us from God and deserves God's punishment of death (Romans 6:23).

God provided. Choose a child to read John 3:16 aloud. Say that God sent His Son Jesus, the perfect solution to our sin problem, to rescue us from the punishment we deserve. It's something we, as sinners, could never earn on our own. Jesus alone saves us. Read and explain Ephesians 2:8-9.

Jesus gives. Share with kids that Jesus lived a perfect life, died on the cross for our sins, and rose again. Because Jesus gave up His life for us, we can be welcomed into God's family for eternity. This is the best gift ever! Read Romans 5:8, 2 Corinthians 5:21, or 1 Peter 3:18.

We respond. Tell kids that they can respond to Jesus. Read Romans 10:9-10,13. Review these aspects of our response: Believe in your heart that Jesus alone saves you through what He's already done on the cross. Repent, turning from self and sin to Jesus. Tell God and others that your faith is in Jesus.

Offer to talk with any child who is interested in responding to Jesus.

Small Group LEADER

Session Title: Joshua and Caleb
Bible Passage: Numbers 13:1–14:38
Big Picture Question: What happens when God's people sin? Sin has a price, but God forgives when people seek forgiveness.
Key Passage: Exodus 20:1-17
Unit Christ Connection: God instructed His covenant people how to live holy lives in an unholy world. This sustained their relationship with God until the perfect plan was revealed through Jesus Christ.

• Key Passage Slides or Posters (enhanced CD)
• dry erase board and markers (optional)
• medium-sized ball

Key passage activity (5 minutes)

Make sure the key passage, Exodus 20:1-17, is visible for each child, either as the printed posters or written on a dry erase board. Read the passage together.

Say • The Ten Commandments were God's rules of how the Israelites could live a holy life. They continued to fail at keeping God's commands. Each time, God forgave the people, but they still had consequences or a price to pay. *What happens when God's people sin? Sin has a price, but God forgives when people seek forgiveness.* Let's see if we can remember the commands God gave Israel.

Invite the kids to form a circle. Choose a volunteer to hold a medium-sized ball that bounces. Direct the volunteer to say the first commandment and bounce the ball to another kid. Whoever gets the ball must say the next commandment. If the kid with the ball doesn't know the next commandment, he may say "help." He will pass the ball to someone volunteering to help. If he does know the next commandment, he says it and passes it to whomever he wishes.

• Bibles, 1 per kid
• Small Group Visual Pack
• Big Picture Question Slide or Poster (enhanced CD)

Bible story review (10 minutes)

Encourage the kids to find Numbers 13 in their Bibles. Help them as needed.

Say • Is Numbers in the New Testament or Old Testament? (*Old Testament*) What books come before and after Numbers? (*Leviticus, Deuteronomy*) Which division of the Bible is Numbers in? (*Law*) What are the other books of Law? (*Genesis, Exodus, Leviticus, Deuteronomy*) Numbers tells us how the Israelites refused to take the promised land and how they wandered in the wilderness because of their sin.

Use the small group visual pack to show kids where today's Bible story is on the timeline. Use the short monologue below from Joshua to review the story. Ask someone to be ready to play his part or consider a simple, quick clothing change before reading—even something as simple as wrapping a towel around your head.

Joshua: I was part of a group of 12 who were called to go see the land God had promised us. We traveled around the land for 40 days. It was even more wonderful than I had imagined! The land was covered in green, a far cry from the desert we'd been traveling through. There was food like I'd never seen. There were grapes the size of your hand! We got back to the people, and Caleb told everyone we should take the land.

I was so excited, and I thought everyone would agree. However, the other spies started complaining about the people there. They said they were like giants. The people believed them and complained all night. They were ready to find a new leader and go back to Egypt.

Caleb and I tried to tell them God is on our side, so we can't lose. Moses told us later that God was angry but agreed to forgive us. I was sad though, because Moses

said that only Caleb and I would live to see and go into in the land. If only the people had believed and trusted God!

Say • Do you always trust God? When we don't trust God, we sin. By refusing to go into the land, the people were saying God would not keep His promise. It's easy to see why God was upset. Aren't you thankful that God forgives us when we sin?

Show the big picture question slide or poster.

Say • That reminds me of our big picture question. *What happens when God's people sin? Sin has a price, but God forgives when people seek forgiveness.*

Activity choice (10 minutes)

• tape

Option 1: Grasshopper races

Tape a long start line and a long finish line several feet apart. Explain to the kids that you are going to run grasshopper races. Choose three or four kids to race from the start line to the finish line. They must race by hopping on all fours. In each hop, their hands must touch the ground. Anything other than a hop disqualifies them. If you have several kids, run several races. Let the winners compete for the grasshopper championship.

Say • Instead of seeing how big God was, the Israelites only saw how big the people were in the land God promised them. They sinned against God. *What happens when God's people sin? Sin has a price, but God forgives when people seek forgiveness.*

• clothespin, 1 per kid
• chenille stem, 1 per 2 kids
• crayons, markers, or paint

Option 2: Grasshopper clothespin

Distribute a clothespin and half a piece of a chenille stem to each kid. Allow kids to color or paint the clothespin green. Color eyes on the end of the clothespin that opens. Demonstrate how to open the clothespin and insert the chenille stem about halfway. Close the clothespin, pinching the chenille stem. Fold the chenille stem on each side of the clothespin to form legs.

Say • Instead of seeing how big God is, the Israelites only saw how big the people were in the land God promised them. They sinned against God. *What happens when God's people sin? Sin has a price, but God forgives when people seek forgiveness.*

Journal and Prayer (5 minutes)

• folder, 1 per kid
• Journal Page, 1 per kid (enhanced CD)
• markers or crayons
• Bible Story Coloring Page

Distribute each child's journal and the journal page provided with this session. Instruct the kids to draw their favorite fruit. Older kids can share a time they forgave someone who did something wrong to them.

Say • Here's one last look at our big picture question. *What happens when God's people sin? Sin has a price, but God forgives when people seek forgiveness.*

Make sure each child puts this week's sheet in his journal and then collect them. Keep the journals in the classroom so they will be available every week or as often as you wish to use them.

If time remains, take prayer requests or allow kids to color the coloring page provided with this session. End the session with prayer, thanking God for His forgiveness when we seek it. Pray for each child by name, and ask God to help us always follow His direction.

Teacher BIBLE STUDY

The Israelites had been wandering in the wilderness when they started to complain to Moses and to God. God had done some pretty amazing things for the Israelites—He rescued them from the hand of Pharaoh, He parted the Red Sea so they could safely cross, and He provided manna for them to eat. But to the Israelites, it wasn't good enough.

God punished them because He knew their dissatisfaction was a sign of a bigger issue: a heart problem—a sin problem. They stopped believing that God was good. In their hearts, the Israelites believed the same lie that rattled Eve in the garden. Maybe God isn't interested in giving us what is best. Maybe He is holding out on us. God sent poisonous snakes that bit the people and killed many of them. The Israelites repented. They wanted Moses to ask God to take away the snakes.

God provided a solution: "Make a snake image out of bronze and mount it on a pole. When anyone who is bitten looks at it, he will recover."

In John 3:14, Jesus said, "Just as Moses lifted up the snake in the wilderness, so the Son of Man must be lifted up." What was Jesus talking about?

God put Jesus in the position of the snake; Jesus was lifted high on the cross. So Jesus invites us, "Turn to Me and be saved, all the ends of the earth. For I am God, and there is no other" (Isaiah 45:22).

As you teach kids, emphasize the problem that all of us face: we are sick with sin and deserve death. Then rejoice with them over the solution: Jesus, the sinless Savior, became sin for us and was lifted up on the cross in our place. We must do nothing but look to Him to be saved.

Younger Kids BIBLE STUDY OVERVIEW

Session Title: The Bronze Snake
Bible Passage: Numbers 17:1-12; 20:1-12,14-20; 21:4-9
Big Picture Question: What happens when people repent from sin? Sin comes with consequences, but God provides the way of salvation.
Key Passage: Exodus 20:1-17
Unit Christ Connection: God instructed His covenant people how to live holy lives in an unholy world. This sustained their relationship with God until the perfect plan was revealed through Jesus Christ.

Small Group Opening

Large Group Leader

Small Group Leader

The Wilderness

The BIBLE STORY

The Bronze Snake
Numbers 17:1-12; 20:1-12,14-20; 21:4-9

After the Israelites did not go into the promised land, they had to wander in the wilderness as punishment. Along the way, the Israelites grumbled and complained. First, they complained, "We don't need Moses and Aaron to tell us what to do!" God said that one man from each of the 12 tribes was to bring his staff to the tabernacle, including Aaron. They put Aaron's name on his staff. God said, "The staff of the man I choose will sprout, and that will stop the complaints the Israelites have made about you." The next morning, Aaron's staff not only sprouted, but it also formed buds, grew flowers, and produced almonds! God was showing the Israelites that He chose Aaron to serve Him.

Next, they complained that they did not have any water to drink at Meribah. God told Moses and Aaron to stand in front of all the people and speak to a rock, to make the waters come out of the rock. Moses was angry with the people, though, and he didn't listen to God. Instead of talking to the rock, Moses hit the rock two times. The water came out, but God was angry that Moses and Aaron did not obey. God said because they did not obey, they could not go into the promised land.

Then they traveled from Mount Hor (HAWR), going by the Red Sea so they wouldn't have to travel through the land of Edom (EE duhm). Even though Moses had asked Edom if they could pass through—the Israelites said they would pay Edom for using any food or water—the people of Edom said, "No!" So the Israelites had to travel around Edom.

God had provided for His people, but the journey was long, and the Israelites became impatient. They grumbled and complained to God and Moses, "Why have you led us out here from Egypt to die in the wilderness? We have no bread or water! The food we have is no good!"

God sent poisonous snakes against the Israelites, and the snakes bit many of them. Many of the Israelites died. The people realized they had sinned by complaining to God. So they told Moses, "We know we have sinned. Please ask God to take the snakes away." Moses interceded for the people. He spoke to God for them.

God told Moses, "Make a snake image and put it on a pole. When anyone who is bitten looks at it, he will recover." Moses made a bronze snake and mounted it on a pole. Whenever someone was bitten, he looked at the bronze snake, and he recovered. Even when the Israelites sinned against God by not trusting Him to take care of them, God still loved them. He had to punish their sins, but He also helped heal them.

Christ Connection: The Israelites faced a huge problem because of their sin. God sent snakes to punish them. Anyone who was bitten could look at the snake on the pole and not die. Because of our sin, we face a huge problem: we are separated from God. We deserve to die. Anyone who looks to Jesus on the cross and trusts in Him will be saved and be made right with God.

Small Group OPENING

Session Title: The Bronze Snake
Bible Passage: Numbers 17:1-12; 20:1-12,14-20; 21:4-9
Big Picture Question: What happens when people repent from sin? Sin comes with consequences, but God provides the way of salvation.
Key Passage: Exodus 20:1-17
Unit Christ Connection: God instructed His covenant people how to live holy lives in an unholy world. This sustained their relationship with God until the perfect plan was revealed through Jesus Christ.

Welcome time

Arriving Activity: I'm sorry

Engage kids in conversation as they enter the room.

Talk about the words, "I'm sorry." Share a time you did something wrong and asked someone to forgive you. Allow the kids to share, too.

Say • Sometimes we need to seek forgiveness. We can't take back what we do that is wrong, but we can seek forgiveness. God also wants His people to realize when they sin and seek His forgiveness. We'll see an example of that in today's Bible story.

Activity page (5 minutes)

• "Complaint List" activity page, 1 per kid
• pencils

Guide boys and girls to complete the activity page.

Say • We often complain when we don't like something. We'll see in today's Bible story that God is not happy when we complain.

Session starter (10 minutes)

Option 1: Real leader

Invite the kids to sit in a large circle. Choose one volunteer to leave the room or turn from the group. Choose another kid to be the "secret leader." It will only be a secret to the first volunteer. The rest of the kids must follow the motions of the "secret leader." Encourage them not to look directly at the "secret leader" or tell the first volunteer who he is. The "secret leader" should start a new motion every few seconds. Invite the first volunteer to watch the group and try to figure out who the "secret leader" is. Repeat as time allows.

Say • Each time someone was tested to see if he could figure out who the leader was. Today's Bible story has another test that will determine who would lead the Israelites.

• toy snakes

Option 2: Snake game

Form small groups with the same number of kids lined up single file. Each team needs to have a rubber snake or water snake (plastic toy filled with water). The first kid in line must pass the snake to the second kid in line and continue to the end of the line. Each kid must spin around 360 degrees before handing it to the next kid. The first team to get their snake to the end of the line is the winner. Repeat as time allows.

Say • This was a fun game because the snakes are not real. Imagine being surrounded by real snakes. That's what happened to the Israelites in today's Bible story.

Transition to large group

Large Group LEADER

Session Title: The Bronze Snake
Bible Passage: Numbers 17:1-12; 20:1-12,14-20; 21:4-9
Big Picture Question: What happens when people repent from sin? Sin comes with consequences, but God provides the way of salvation.
Key Passage: Exodus 20:1-17
Unit Christ Connection: God instructed His covenant people how to live holy lives in an unholy world. This sustained their relationship with God until the perfect plan was revealed through Jesus Christ.

• countdown video

Countdown

Show the countdown video as your kids arrive, and set it to end as large group time begins.

• toy snake

Introduce the session (1 minute)

[Large group leader enters with a rubber, plastic, or wooden snake.]

Leader • This is actually something you might expect to find in the desert. Most snakes love warm weather, so the desert is a perfect place for them. How many of you would like to come face-to-face with a real snake? Maybe you would, but I wouldn't. Snakes can bite you, and some snake bites can really hurt you. Today we will see how God used a bunch of snakes to teach some complaining people a lesson.

• Timeline Map

Timeline map (1 minute)

Leader • Let's take a look back at what's happened during the last few weeks. The new nation of Israel, God's chosen people, had been freed from slavery in Egypt. God led them out, divided the Red Sea, destroyed the Egyptian army, led them by a cloud during the day and a fire at night, gave them 10 rules, and talked to them directly and through Moses. God even stayed with them in the tabernacle He had them build. This should have been evidence that God was keeping the promise He first made to Abraham. After all of that, though, the people still questioned God's promise, His choice of leaders, and the way He took care of them. God forgave them, but they still had to face consequences or pay for their sins. The title is "The Bronze Snake." A bronze snake on a pole. That should be interesting.

Big picture question (1 minute)

Leader • The Bible has all kinds of interesting stories. More importantly, the Bible tells us the story of God's plan to save us from sin through Jesus. That's why I always ask you if you brought your Bible. God wants you to know His plan. So, here we go. If you have your Bible, let everyone see it. Great!

Now let's look at our big picture question. ***What happens when people repent from sin?***

Sing (5 minutes)

• "Give You Glory" song

Leader • *Repent* means to turn or change from disobeying God to obeying God. The Israelites had started a pattern of not obeying God. When God's people disobey Him, they don't give God the glory He deserves. God wants all of His people to give Him glory.

Sing together "Give You Glory."

Key passage (4 minutes)

• "Ten Commandments" song
• Key Passage Slides or Posters (enhanced CD)

Leader • The last time the Israelites disobeyed or sinned against God, they were told they would not get to live in the wonderful land God was going to give them. Instead they would spend the next 40 years in the desert. No matter what, they still broke the 10 rules we call the Ten Commandments. Let's see if you remember those commands.

Show the slide or poster of this unit's key passage, Exodus 20:1-17. Lead the boys and girls to read the key passage together.

Leader • Each time the people broke these commands, Moses pleaded with God to forgive them. God forgave them each time. Let's see if we know the Ten Commandments by singing them together.

Sing together "Ten Commandments."

Tell the Bible story (10 minutes)

- "The Bronze Snake" video
- Bibles, 1 per kid
- Bible Story Picture Slide or Poster (enhanced CD)

Leader • As we come to our Bible story, the Israelites are stuck in the wilderness. We wonder about several things as we get ready to open our Bibles. What would they do in the desert? Had they learned their lesson, and our big picture question, *what happens when people repent from sin?*

Open your Bible to Numbers 17. Choose to tell the Bible story in your own words using the script provided, or show the "The Bronze Snake" video.

Leader • God's people started complaining about everything. They didn't like having Moses and Aaron as their leaders, so God made it clear that Moses and Aaron were the leaders He had chosen.

They complained about food and water. Their complaining made Moses so angry that he disobeyed God's instructions on how to get them water. This disobedience meant Moses and Aaron would not get to enter the promised land after their 40 years in the desert.

The people then complained about their time in the

desert and the food God gave them. God finally sent poisonous snakes that bit the people, and many of them died. This was a consequence or punishment because they continued to sin against God. The people finally understood that they had sinned and asked Moses to seek God's forgiveness for them. ***What happens when people repent from sin? Sin comes with consequences, but God provides the way of salvation.*** *Salvation* means God's rescue from sin.

Moses told God the people had repented. God told him to put a snake image on a pole. He told Moses to tell the people to look at the image if they were bitten. Then, they would live. Moses made a bronze snake and put it on a pole. It worked just as God said.

Ask the following review questions:

1. What did God say would happen to the staff of the man He chose as leader of the people? (*It would sprout or bud, Numbers 17:5*)

2. What did Moses do that kept him from getting to one day enter the promise land? (*disobeyed God by hitting the rock instead of talking to it, Numbers 20:8-12*)

3. What did God do to punish the Israelites because of their sin? (*He sent poisonous snakes, Numbers 21:6*)

4. When the people repented what did God do? (*He saved them by telling them to look at a pole with a snake on it, Numbers 21:8-9*)

5. Who do we look to when we sin? (*Jesus*)

Discussion starter video (4 minutes)

• "Lost and Found" video

Leader • Have you ever been in a situation where it looked like there was no way out? Maybe you felt like this.

Play "Lost and Found."

Leader • Have you ever thought you were lost before? How did you react and what did you do? Sometimes you don't understand how important it is to know someone is taking care of you until that person is gone and you are alone feeling helpless.

The Israelites complained over and over about the way God cared for them, so He gave them what they wanted. He stopped. When He sent the snakes, the people understood how God had really taken care of them. They realized they had sinned and repented. ***What happens when people repent from sin? Sin comes with consequences, but God provides the way of salvation.***

For the people, there was no way out. Only God could save them. God gave what would seem like a strange suggestion. Look to something else. It was as if the snake on a pole would take their punishment. It's the same way with sin. We have no way to defeat sin. God instead gave us someone who could defeat sin. The only way we can be saved is to look to Jesus, trusting Him as our Savior.

The Gospel: God's Plan for Me (optional)

Use Scripture and the guide provided with this session to explain to boys and girls how to become a Christian. Assign individuals to meet with kids who have more questions. If this is not possible, encourage boys and girls to ask their parents, small group leaders, and other Christian adults any questions they may have about becoming a Christian.

- **God rules.** God created and is in charge of everything. (Gen. 1:1; Rev. 4:11; Col. 1:16-17)
- **We sinned.** Since Adam and Eve, everyone has chosen to disobey God. (Rom. 3:23; 6:23)

- **God provided.** God sent His Son Jesus to rescue us from the punishment we deserve. (John 3:16; Eph. 2:8-9)
- **Jesus gives.** Jesus lived a perfect life, died on the cross for our sins, and rose again so we can be welcomed into God's family. (Rom. 5:8; 2 Cor. 5:21; 1 Pet. 3:18)
- **We respond.** Believe that Jesus alone saves you. Repent. Tell God that your faith is in Jesus. (Rom. 10:9-10,13)

Prayer (4 minutes)

• Big Picture Question Slide or Poster (enhanced CD)

Show the big picture question slide or poster.

Leader • Let's test what you remember with our big picture question. ***What happens when people repent from sin? Sin comes with consequences, but God provides the way of salvation.***

Ask again for those who are afraid of snakes. Invite them to say the big picture question and the other kids to answer. Swap roles and repeat.

Before transitioning to small group, make any necessary announcements. Lead the kids in prayer. Thank God for His way of salvation, and pray that kids will be thankful for what God has given them instead of complaining about it.

Dismiss to small groups

Small Group LEADER

Session Title: The Bronze Snake
Bible Passage: Numbers 17:1-12; 20:1-12,14-20; 21:4-9
Big Picture Question: What happens when people repent from sin? Sin comes with consequences, but God provides the way of salvation.
Key Passage: Exodus 20:1-17
Unit Christ Connection: God instructed His covenant people how to live holy lives in an unholy world. This sustained their relationship with God until the perfect plan was revealed through Jesus Christ.

• Key Passage
Slides or Posters
(enhanced CD)
• dry erase board and
markers (optional)

Key passage activity (5 minutes)

Make sure the key passage, Exodus 20:1-17, is visible for each child, either as the printed posters or written on a dry erase board. Read the passage together.

Say • These were commandments God gave the people, so they could be together with God. The people learned that they had to face consequences for their sin, a punishment. Still, God showed love for His people because He rescued His people from sin. *What happens when people repent from sin? Sin comes with consequences, but God provides the way of salvation.* Let's see how well you know the Ten Commandments.

Explain to the kids that you are going to clap somewhere between 1 to 10 times, and you want to see who can say the commandment that goes with the number of claps the fastest. Whoever wins the first round gets to clap for the next commandment. Continue playing until all the commandments have been said or until ready to start the review.

Bible story review (10 minutes)

- Bibles, 1 per kid
- Small Group Visual Pack
- Big Picture Question Slide or Poster (enhanced CD)

Encourage the kids to find Numbers 21 in their Bibles. Help them as needed.

Say • Is Numbers in the New Testament or Old Testament? (*Old Testament*) What book comes before Numbers? (*Leviticus*) Which division of the Bible is Numbers in? (*Law*) What are the other books of Law? (*Genesis, Exodus, Leviticus, Deuteronomy*) What does Numbers tell us about? (*Numbers tells us about the Israelites' rejection of the promised land and the years they wandered in the wilderness because of their sin.*)

Use the small group visual pack to show kids where today's Bible story is on the timeline. Review the Bible story provided or summarize the story in your own words. Below is a list of complaints from the Israelites. Invite the kids to talk about whether they sometimes complain about the same things. Some possible questions are provided.

- They complained about their leaders. Do you ever complain about your parents, teachers, or older brothers and sisters who are allowed to be in charge?
- They complained about what they had to drink. Have you ever complained about being thirsty or having to drink one thing when you wanted another?
- They complained about where they were and where they had to go. Have you ever complained about not wanting to go somewhere you were supposed to go?
- They complained about food. How many of you have ever complained about what you had to eat?

Say • We have all complained about at least one of these things. It may seem mean of God to send poisonous snakes to the people. He wasn't trying to be mean. He was trying to show them their sin and that sin has

a price. They looked to the snake on the pole like we look to Jesus. We can do nothing but trust in what He has already done.

Show the big picture question slide or poster.

Say • Here's comes our big picture question and answer. *What happens when people repent from sin? Sin comes with consequences, but God provides the way of salvation.*

Activity choice (10 minutes)

Option 1: Snake tag

Create a snake pit by making a large circle with tape. Choose a volunteer to be the snake. The snake goes to the middle of the circle. All the kids gather in the circle around the snake. All the kids must crawl during the game, including the snake. The leader will yell "snake!" When she does, the snake may start tagging kids. The goal is for the kids to get out of the pit before being tagged.

• tape

Say • When God sent snakes to bite the Israelites, they realized they had sinned and repented. *What happens when people repent from sin? Sin comes with consequences, but God provides the way of salvation.*

Option 2: Snake Spring

• green paper, 1 per kid
• pen or pencil, 1 per kid
• scissors, 1 per kid

Provide a piece of paper, a pen or pencil, and a pair of scissors for each kid. Demonstrate how to put the pencil in the middle of the paper and begin to make a large swirl pattern, like a snail shell. The pattern will eventually run off the paper. Cut along the line to create a snake. The middle part is the head. Cut the excess paper off to form the tail. Allow the kids to decorate the snake with eyes and spots.

Say • When God sent snakes to bite the Israelites, they

realized they had sinned and they repented. *What happens when people repent from sin? Sin comes with consequences, but God provides the way of salvation.*

Journal and Prayer (5 minutes)

Distribute each child's journal and the journal page provided with this session. Instruct the kids to draw a snake on a pole. Older kids can share things they complain about but shouldn't.

- folder, 1 per kid
- journal page, 1 per kid (enhanced CD)
- markers or crayons
- Bible story coloring page

Say • Before we go, let's hear the big picture question and answer. *What happens when people repent from sin? Sin comes with consequences, but God provides the way of salvation.*

Make sure each child puts this week's sheet in his journal and then collect them. Keep the journals in the classroom so they will be available every week or as often as you wish to use them.

If time remains, take prayer requests or allow kids to color the coloring page provided with this session. End the session with prayer, thanking God for the way He takes care of us. Pray for each child by name, and ask God to help us trust Him in all things.

Teacher BIBLE STUDY

Balaam was a pagan prophet; he worshiped the gods of the land. People believed that when Balaam cursed or blessed someone, it would be so. Balak, king of Moab, called on Balaam to curse the Israelites because he was afraid they would overtake him and his land. Balak offered a reward to Balaam for his services.

But God spoke to Balaam. God warned Balaam to not curse the Israelites because God had blessed them. Initially, Balaam listened to God, but it's not for nothing that he developed the nickname "the prophet for a profit." Balaam traveled to talk to Balak about the situation. He hoped to get a greater reward from Balak. (See 2 Peter 2:15-16.)

So God sent the Angel of the LORD with a sword to enforce Balaam's obedience. At first, Balaam did not see the Angel, but his donkey did. The donkey stopped three times, and Balaam became so angry that he said, "If I had a sword, I would kill you!" Then God opened Balaam's eyes to the one who did have a sword—the Angel. Balaam realized his sin and said to God, "If you want me to go back home, I will."

God gave Balaam permission to continue as long as he spoke only the words God gave him. Balaam obeyed God; he spoke in four clear messages, insisting that God would bless the Israelites. One of the ways God would bless the Israelites is found in Numbers 24:17: "A star will come from Jacob, and a scepter will arise from Israel." This prophecy referred to and was fulfilled by Jesus.

Today you have the opportunity to teach kids that God protects His people. Not even a pagan prophet could speak against the blessing of God. God's promises are sure. We can trust that God is who He says He is, and that He will do what He says He will do.

Younger Kids BIBLE STUDY OVERVIEW

Session Title: Balaam
Bible Passage: Numbers 22:1–24:25
Big Picture Question: Who protected God's people? God protected His people from their enemies.
Key Passage: Exodus 20:1-17
Unit Christ Connection: God instructed His covenant people how to live holy lives in an unholy world. This sustained their relationship with God until the perfect plan was revealed through Jesus Christ.

Small Group Opening

Large Group Leader

Small Group Leader

The BIBLE STORY

Balaam

Numbers 22:1–24:25

The Israelites had wandered in the desert for 40 years. Finally, they had come to the edge of the promised land. They camped in the plains of Moab (MOH ab) near the Jordan River. By now, all of the old men had died except for Moses, Joshua, and Caleb.

Now Balak (BAY lak), the king of Moab, saw the Israelites and was afraid. If the Israelites moved into Moab, they would take over! King Balak knew of a wise man named Balaam (BAY luhm). He sent his messengers to Balaam and said, "Come and curse the Israelites so that I might be able to defeat them." The king knew that whomever Balaam cursed became cursed, and whomever he blessed became blessed.

Balaam said, "I'm not sure if God wants me to go with you. Wait here overnight." During the night, God said to Balaam, "Don't go with these men. Do not curse the Israelites, because they are blessed."

The next day, Balaam told the men, "God doesn't want me to go with you." So the messengers went back to King Balak and gave him the message. The king pleaded with Balaam again. "Please come curse these people! I will do whatever you ask me."

"I cannot go against the LORD's commands," Balaam replied to the messengers. "Stay here overnight and I will see what God wants me to do." That night, God spoke to Balaam again. "Go with the men this time when they call you," God said. "But only do what I tell you to do."

The next morning, Balaam got up and saddled his donkey. When Balaam left with the men, God sent an angel to stop Balaam. Balaam could not see the angel, but his donkey could.

Three times the angel stood in the way, and three times the donkey stopped. First the donkey went off the road. Then she ran into a wall. Finally, she lay down on the ground. Balaam didn't understand why the donkey was stopping. He hit the donkey when she stopped, so God gave the donkey the ability to speak.

"What have I done to you that you have beaten me three times?" the donkey said.

Balaam was so mad that he didn't even wonder why his donkey was talking! "You made me look like a fool!" Balaam said. "I should kill you!"

God allowed Balaam to see the angel, and Balaam said, "I have sinned! I will go back if you want me to."

The angel said, "No, go with these men. But only say what I tell you to say."

King Balak saw Balaam coming and said, "What took you so long?" Balaam explained, "I cannot say anything I want to you. I can only say what God tells me to say.

The next morning, the king took Balaam to see where the Israelites were camping. Balaam went to a nearby hill and God talked to him. Balaam returned to the king and told him that he could not curse someone whom God had blessed. Instead, he blessed the Israelites.

The king was not happy! But Balaam said, "I can only say what God puts in my mouth."

King Balak took Balaam to another place to look out over the Israelites. God met with Balaam and gave him another message. Again, Balaam blessed the Israelites. He even told the king that the Israelites would defeat him!

"If you won't curse them, don't say anything!" King Balak said. A third time, the king took Balaam to a place overlooking the Israelites. God gave Balaam a third message. Again, Balaam blessed the Israelites.

The king had heard enough! "I brought you here to curse the Israelites, but you have blessed them three times!" he said. "Go home!"

Before Balaam went home, he had another message for the king. Balaam's fourth message was special because he said that one day the Lord would be born to the people of Israel. It was a special promise that went like this: "I see him, but not now; I perceive him, but not near. A star will come from Jacob, and a scepter will arise from Israel." After Balaam had said these things, he went home.

Christ Connection: Fourteen hundred years after Balaam announced Jesus' birth, wise men followed a star to the place where Jesus was born. The wise men worshiped Jesus as King. (Matthew 2:2)

Small Group OPENING

Session Title: Balaam
Bible Passage: Numbers 22:1–24:25
Big Picture Question: Who protected God's people? God protected His people from their enemies.
Key Passage: Exodus 20:1-17
Unit Christ Connection: God instructed His covenant people how to live holy lives in an unholy world. This sustained their relationship with God until the perfect plan was revealed through Jesus Christ.

Welcome time

Arriving Activity: Animal fun
As kids arrive, ask the kids if they could be any animal, what would they be? Ask each one to either make the noise that animal would make or act like that animal. Encourage them to go around the room guessing what animal each kid is representing.

Say • Now imagine if you were an animal that could talk. Does that sound impossible? It happened. Find out which animal talked and how in just a few minutes.

Activity page (5 minutes)

• "Common Things" activity page, 1 per kid
• pencils

Guide boys and girls to complete the activity page.

Say • All these items are used to protect us. Today we will find out another way we are protected.

Session starter (10 minutes)

Option 1: Donkey call
Secretly choose one kid to be a donkey. Choose another volunteer to find the donkey. The volunteer must say "Hee" and the donkey must say "Haw." Encourage the kids to protect the donkey by making other animal noises. Once the

volunteer finds the donkey, the donkey becomes the next volunteer. Choose another secret donkey, and play again.

Say • You all tried to protect a donkey. In today's Bible story we will find a donkey who protects somebody.

Option 2: Donkey rides

• chairs, 2
• tape
• yardsticks, dowel rods, or broom handles; 1 per group

Tape two start lines side by side, and place a chair several feet from each line. Make sure to leave enough space between each start line and chair for kids to move without colliding. Form two groups, and instruct each group to line up single file behind one of the start lines. Give the first kid in each line a yardstick, dowel rod, or broom handle. Explain that they are going to be in a donkey rodeo. Each one is to ride a "donkey," the yardstick, to the chair, around it, and back to the start line. At that point, he must hand the donkey to the next kid in line, who does the same thing. Continue until everyone has ridden in the donkey rodeo. The first team to finish the donkey rodeo is the winner.

Say • Today's story has a donkey that's not in a rodeo, but it does have a long ride ahead and a very strange story to tell.

Transition to large group

Large Group LEADER

Session Title: Balaam
Bible Passage: Numbers 22:1–24:25
Big Picture Question: Who protected God's people? God protected His people from their enemies.
Key Passage: Exodus 20:1-17
Unit Christ Connection: God instructed His covenant people how to live holy lives in an unholy world. This sustained their relationship with God until the perfect plan was revealed through Jesus Christ.

• countdown video

Countdown

Show the countdown video as your kids arrive, and set it to end as large group time begins.

• stuffed donkey or picture of a donkey

Introduce the session (1 minute)

[Large group leader enters with a donkey stuffed animal or picture.]

Leader • How many of you know what I have with me today? It's a donkey. Donkeys are great animals to have in the desert. They are strong, smart, and able to deal with dry weather. Lots of stories in the Bible deal with a donkey because donkeys were the cars and trucks for most people during Bible times. Today's story is very unique, though. We even get to see a donkey talk.

• Timeline Map

Timeline map (1 minute)

Leader • Things had not gone as planned for the Israelites and their new nation. God performed miracles, took care of them, and led them right up to the land He promised they would have more than 400 years before. They were scared of the people there, so they refused to go in. Worst of all, the people almost always complained. God still showed love for His people and forgave them of their sins when they repented and turned back to Him. Israel couldn't see how blessed they were, but other nations were taking notice.

Big picture question (1 minute)

Leader • It's great to see the story of the Bible come together right before your eyes. It's important to remember that these stories are not just stories. They are real events. Today's story seems like something you might only see at the movies or read about in a fairy tale, but it really happened. God can do anything, and the story we are about to see is proof of that. The only way you can see this story is with your Bible. You know what that means. It's Bible check time! Let's see those Bibles.

Keep in mind that your Bible has the answer to our big picture question. ***Who protected God's people?***

Sing (5 minutes)

• "Give You Glory" song

Leader • Have you ever been scared of something? Maybe you are afraid of the dark, dogs, or being alone. The Israelites were afraid of how big the people were in the promised land, the land God planned for them to live in. Then they chose to complain about what God had given them when God wanted them to give Him glory for all He had done.

Sing together "Give You Glory."

Key passage (4 minutes)

• "Ten Commandments" song
• Key Passage Slides or Posters (enhanced CD)

Leader • For the last several weeks, we have talked about the commands God gave to His people—commands they continued to break. The Ten Commandments are a great reminder that we can't always keep God's law, but when

The Wilderness

we trust in Jesus, we want to give Him glory through obedience to Him. Let's see if you can say our key passage, the Ten Commandments, from memory.

Show the slide or poster of this unit's key passage, Exodus 20:1-17. Hide it if you think the kids know it already. Lead the boys and girls to say the key passage together.

Leader • It's OK if you still don't have them all down. Maybe our key passage song will help.

Sing together "Ten Commandments."

Tell the Bible story (10 minutes)

Leader • Get ready to open your Bible and see what amazing thing God did. You are about to be reminded that God can do anything and that He loves to bless His people. You'll also see that when you find the answer to our big picture question. *Who protected God's people?*

Open your Bible to Numbers 22. Choose to tell the Bible story in your own words using the script provided, or show the "Balaam" video.

Leader • The time had come for the Israelites to move into the land God had promised them. It had been 40 years since they had rejected God by refusing to go into the promised land the first time they came to the border.

The king of a nation living in that land was afraid they would take over, so he went to a man that he thought could curse the Israelites. The man's name was Balaam. Keep in mind, Balaam was not one of God's people. The people he lived among worshiped other gods.

The king sent messengers to Balaam, but God told him not to go and curse the Israelites because God had blessed them. After a second visit, God told Balaam he could go as long as he did only what God asked him to do.

• "Balaam" video
• Bibles, 1 per kid
• Bible Story Picture Slide or Poster (enhanced CD)

On the way, an angel tried to stop him, but only his donkey could see the angel. Balaam hit the donkey because he was mad the animal would not keep going. This happened three times, so God gave the donkey the ability to talk. The donkey asked him what she had done to deserve a beating.

Balaam saw the angel. The angel said the donkey had saved his life. Balaam realized that he had sinned and offered to go back. The angel again reminded him that he could go, but he must only say what God told him to say.

Three times the king took him to a place where he could see the Israelites camping, and three times Balaam blessed them instead of cursing them. He even told the king that the Israelites would defeat his people. The king was angry and sent Balaam home.

Before going home, Balaam blessed the Israelities one more time, saying a star would come from Jacob and a king would come from Israel. In the end, God protected His people. ***Who protected God's people? God protected His people from their enemies.***

Ask the following review questions:

1. Why did the king of Moab want to curse the Israelites? (*He was afraid the Israelites might attack and destroy them, Numbers 22:3-6*)

2. What protected Balaam from the angel? (*a donkey, Numbers 22:33*)

3. What did God do when Balaam beat his donkey? (*let the donkey speak, showed him the angel with a sword, Numbers 22:28-31*)

4. What did the angel remind Him about? (*to only say what God told him to, Numbers 22:35*)

5. What did Balaam say would come from Jacob? (*a star, Numbers 24:17*)

Discussion starter video (4 minutes)

- "Protected" video
- Big Picture Question Slide or Poster (enhanced CD)

Leader • The Israelites didn't even know God was protecting them from Balaam. There have probably been times when you have been protected without knowing it, too.

Play "Protected."

Leader • Do you think God has ever protected you without you knowing it? We will see later that the Israelites will find out what happened, but at the moment it happened, nothing in the Bible indicates they knew what Balaam had done at the time. Sometimes bad things happen to us because of sin or because God is using that bad thing for something good we don't know about. However, God is always able to protect us. ***Who protected God's people? God protected His people from their enemies.***

Not only did God use Balaam to bless the Israelities, but Balaam's fourth blessing is very important because it talks about Jesus. Balaam said a star would come from Jacob, and a scepter—a king—would come from Israel. He was talking about something that would happen 1400 years later when a star would guide the wise men to where Jesus was born, and they would worship Him as King.

The Gospel: God's Plan for Me (optional)

Use Scripture and the guide provided with this session to explain to boys and girls how to become a Christian. Assign individuals to meet with kids who have more questions. If this is not possible, encourage boys and girls to ask their parents, small group leaders, and other Christian adults any questions they may have about becoming a Christian.

- **God rules.** God created and is in charge of everything. (Gen. 1:1; Rev. 4:11; Col. 1:16-17)

- **We sinned.** Since Adam and Eve, everyone has chosen to disobey God. (Rom. 3:23; 6:23)
- **God provided.** God sent His Son Jesus to rescue us from the punishment we deserve. (John 3:16; Eph. 2:8-9)
- **Jesus gives.** Jesus lived a perfect life, died on the cross for our sins, and rose again so we can be welcomed into God's family. (Rom. 5:8; 2 Cor. 5:21; 1 Pet. 3:18)
- **We respond.** Believe that Jesus alone saves you. Repent. Tell God that your faith is in Jesus. (Rom. 10:9-10,13)

Prayer (4 minutes)

- Big Picture Question Slide or Poster (enhanced CD)

Show the big picture question slide or poster.

Leader • Who knows the answer to the big picture question? *Who protected God's people? God protected His people from their enemies.*

Encourage the kids to whisper the question and shout the answer. Repeat and challenge the kids to shout the question and whisper the answer.

Before transitioning to small group, make any necessary announcements. Lead the kids in prayer. Thank God for His protection, and pray that kids will understand that God can do anything.

Dismiss to small groups

Small Group LEADER

Session Title: Balaam
Bible Passage: Numbers 22:1–24:25
Big Picture Question: Who protected God's people? God protected His people from their enemies.
Key Passage: Exodus 20:1-17
Unit Christ Connection: God instructed His covenant people how to live holy lives in an unholy world. This sustained their relationship with God until the perfect plan was revealed through Jesus Christ.

- Key Passage Slides or Posters (enhanced CD)
- dry erase board and markers (optional)

Key passage activity (5 minutes)

Make sure the key passage, Exodus 20:1-17, is visible for each child, either as the printed posters or written on a dry erase board. Read the passage together.

Say • No matter how many times the Israelites had already failed to keep His commands, God still protected them when an enemy tried to destroy them. *Who protected God's people? God protected His people from their enemies.* God keeps His promises even when we don't. This is the final week for this key passage, so we will see who knows the Ten Commandments.

Take down the key passage poster. Ask the kids to count with their fingers as you say the Ten Commandments together. Once complete, invite volunteers to try to say all the commandments. They can say them individually or invite a friend to help. Continue as time allows.

- Bibles, 1 per kid
- Small Group Visual Pack
- Big Picture Question Slide or Poster (enhanced CD)

Bible story review (10 minutes)

Encourage the kids to find Numbers 22 in their Bibles. Help them as needed.

Say • Is Numbers in the New Testament or Old Testament?

(*Old Testament*) What book comes before Numbers? (*Leviticus*) Which division of the Bible is Numbers in? (*Law*) What are the other books of Law? (*Genesis, Exodus, Leviticus, Deuteronomy*) What does Numbers tell us about? (*Numbers tells us about the Israelites' rejection of the promised land and the years they wandered in the wilderness because of their sin.*)

Use the small group visual pack to show kids where today's Bible story is on the timeline. Review the Bible story provided or summarize the story in your own words. Explain that a donkey makes the sound "Hee-Haw." As you retell the story, invite the kids to say "Hee-Haw" each time they hear "Balaam."

Say • God protected His people, even if they didn't know it. God kept the same promise He gave to Abraham and the same promise He gave to the Israelites when He freed them from Egypt. God would be their God, and they would be His people.

Show the big picture question slide or poster.

Say • Remember the big picture question and answer. ***Who protected God's people? God protected His people from their enemies.***

Activity choice (10 minutes)

• tape
• sheets of paper, 5 per 2 kids

Option 1: Quick safety

Form groups of two. Tape two long lines 12 feet apart. Designate one line "safety" and the other line "desert." Ask a member from each group to stand on the "safety" line and the other member to stand on the "desert" line across from each other. The kids on the "safety" line get five sheets of paper. Instruct the kids that those on the "safety" line must form a bridge to their partner using the paper. Their partner

is stuck in the desert and needs to be protected from the heat and wild animals. The kids with the paper must lay one piece of paper down and step on it. Lay the next piece down and step on it. Continue until a bridge is formed to their partner. They must use each sheet. Once the bridge is complete, both players must walk on the bridge back to "safety." Give them one minute to get their partner back. Let the kids swap roles and play again. Reduce the amount of time they have as you repeat.

Say • If you were on the "safety" line, you were trying to protect your partner by getting them to safety. We learned today that God protected His people from harm, too. ***Who protected God's people? God protected His people from their enemies.***

Option 2: Donkey mask

- paper plates, 1 per kid
- 8-ounce foam cup, 1 per kid
- crayons
- large craft stick, 1 per kid
- glue
- scissors
- construction paper, brown or gray, 1 per kid

Give each kid a paper plate and an 8-ounce cup. The paper plate will be a donkey mask with the cup as the donkey's nose. Invite the kids to color a mouth on the bottom of the cup and color the rest of the outside of the cup brown or gray. Put glue around the rim of the cup and stick it on the inside of the plate near the bottom but above the rim. Encourage the kids to color eyes just above the cup and color the rest of the inside of the plate the same color as the cup, brown or gray. Invite the kids to cut out long ears using the construction paper, and to glue them above the eyes. Glue a large craft stick on the back for a handle.

Say • God used a talking donkey as He proved He would protect His people. ***Who protected God's people? God protected His people from their enemies.***

Journal and prayer (5 minutes)

- folder, 1 per kid
- Journal Page, 1 per kid (enhanced CD)
- markers or crayons
- Bible Story Coloring Page

Distribute each child's journal and the journal page provided with this session. Instruct the kids to draw a donkey. Older kids can write a way they think God protects them.

Say • Here's one more look at the big picture question. *Who protected God's people? God protected His people from their enemies.*

Make sure each child puts this week's sheet in his journal and collect them. Keep the journals in the classroom so they will be available every week or as often as you wish to use them.

If time remains, take prayer requests or allow kids to color the coloring page provided with this session. End the session with prayer, thanking God for the way He protected the Israelites. Pray for each child by name, and ask God to protect them, too.

Helping Kids Express Their Ideas

During elementary school, kids become inhibited about expressing their thoughts. This lack of response doesn't indicate that fewer ideas or less thinking is going on, but rather they have become more aware of the responses of others.

This hesitation demonstrates their growing concern about what others will think of their ideas, especially their peers. Kids have learned that some of their ideas will not be appreciated or valued by either their teachers or friends. Their concern about the responses to their ideas may make them fearful of sharing their thoughts. But expressing ideas verbally and with others is a very important skill that needs to be nurtured and developed during these years.

A number of approaches exist to assist you in helping your kids feel more comfortable and willing to share their ideas, even with their peers.

Build Trust

When kids are in your classroom, they should recognize it as a place where each child will be respected no matter what is shared. How will kids draw this conclusion? They will know by the way they are greeted when entering your space. When you call their names and inquire about them, is it clear that you are interested in them? Do you make eye contact and really listen to what they say? Do you respond with comments that let them know you hear what they say? Simple words and phrases can help: "Yes, I hear what you are saying." "Hmm, I hadn't thought of that." Over time, they learn by experiences and interactions with you.

During their time with you, kids also learn what others can say in this environment. For example, you might prevent negative responses by saying, "In this classroom, one rule is that you don't criticize others' ideas!" Explain that everyone in the class has good ideas and you want everyone to share their thoughts.

Remember that it takes time to build a supportive environment that will positively impact all of the kids and affect their behaviors.

> It is fine to have moments of silence that allow children to think about their answers.

Ask Questions

Learn to ask questions that have several possible responses, rather than those that have only one correct answer. Ask, "What would you do in this situation?" or "Has this ever happened to you? When?" or "Can you think of other things that we might do?" These open-ended questions allow kids to answer in different ways with each response accepted. Comment on how many different ways a question could be answered. After their responses, you might add your thoughts but not until they have had the opportunity to share their solutions.

Work toward getting all children to contribute a response; don't pressure or embarrass a child who is drawing a blank. In most classes, one or two very verbal children may dominate the conversations. Strive to include all kids, especially the quieter ones, in conversations. You may need to limit the talkative child by saying, "We are listening to Sarah now." Sometimes, a shy child will not answer in a group but will share thoughts with you privately or with another child. Remember, this is an early step in getting this child involved in communicating his or her thoughts. Treasure it and recognize it as a way of moving toward more active participation.

Give Time

Giving kids time to respond to questions or to come up with a plan of action is important. Often, teachers don't like silence when asking a question. That long pause seems negative. Teachers tend to jump in and give the answer. Most children, especially creative thinkers, need time to review their options and come up with the one

> Kids build confidence by making choices and determining what they do.

they want to share. If the teacher answers questions too quickly, children learn to not respond because their answers are not necessary. Try to pause and wait patiently until an answer or suggestion is given. Then, support the idea. It is fine to have moments of silence that allow children to think about their answers.

Work in Small Groups

Most kids will talk more when working on a project in small groups. Speaking is far less threatening in a small group than in a large group with many people listening. Think of ways to divide the large group into smaller working groups and assign each group a specific task. When sufficient time has been given for group work, regroup and let the groups share what they have done. On chart paper, write what each group concluded and add the names of every person in the group. This helps each child see that he was a contributing member to the discussion. Small groups are a great way to organize activities in the classroom while encouraging collaboration.

Give Choices

Kids build confidence by making choices and determining what they do. We want kids to be competent decision-makers. In your classroom, are they trusted to think and choose things that interest them? When kids are trusted to think and choose, they gain confidence and are more willing to try new things or express their ideas.

Although the teacher directs a significant part of the classroom, kids also have many opportunities to make decisions and influence what happens. Ask: "What art materials will you use to create your picture? Where would you like to sit? Who will you work with on a project? How can

you show your family what you learned today?" Kids learn to make good choices by having many opportunities to practice making decisions.

Plan Refection Time

In our busy world, we have little time to reflect on what we did or how things progressed. Today's kids need time to talk together, to discuss issues, and to determine what they have accomplished. At the end of your time together, take a moment to talk about what happened. What questions do they have or what did they find out?

These gathering times build a sense of community and help establish a place with people who care and support each child.

For kids to express their thoughts and ideas, you must demonstrate that what they say is important to you. If you support and value their comments, questions, and efforts, they will participate without fear or worry of criticism. This positive and supportive environment will help them build confidence and the ability to express what they think.

Excerpted from *in mINistry with kids*, volume 5, number 1.

I Need That

We spend time every year talking with kids about the difference between wants and needs. Sometimes we see something in a store or a catalogue and say, "I need that," when what we really mean is "I want that." But there are things that we really need to be healthy and successful.

Being aware of kids' needs is an important part of transformational teaching: teaching to change lives. Jesus always met people's needs as He taught and sought to lead them in a new direction. Knowing kids' needs is important if you want to communicate God's truth.

Kids need security

Girls and boys need to feel that they can depend on adults. That is why it is so important for adults to be committed and to regularly attend. Let the children know that you'll be there and that they can trust you as a leader and a friend.

Kids need acceptance

Kids need to feel as if they are loved no matter what. The "no matter what" part can be difficult because you may have times when you want to go hide in the supply closet! But every child needs to hear a message of grace. God accepts and loves children. We must accept them and love them with God's kind of love.

Kids need guidance

Tied to acceptance is guidance. Boys and girls are in a constant state of change. They are growing and trying new things. They are a bundle of emotions and energy. What they need you to be— whether they admit it or not—is a Christian adult who will gently, but firmly, establish limits and consistently give guidance to their experiences at church.

Kids also need independence

Growth is the process of moving from dependence to independence. (My friend's 3-year-old grandson already feels those urges. His favorite statement is "I do it myself!")

Sure—you can write a better song. You can make a nicer looking picture. But kids want to do their own work. They need

Younger Kids Bible Study Leader Guide

opportunities to do as much as possible for themselves.

Kids need practice in making choices

We desperately want kids to learn how to make good choices for themselves. They need to practice. Give boys and girls appropriate opportunities to choose and make decisions.

Kids need to achieve and feel successful

Kids need to have opportunities to do things well and to see that they are growing. What may seem to be a small accomplishment to us may be huge to them. Praise them for their achievements. Remember to keep compliments honest: Kids know if you are being real.

Kids need biblical leaders

Keep in mind that the greatest thing you can do for your kids is to be an authentic Christian, an example, and a biblical leader. Give girls and boys the love, tenderness, respect, and honesty that they truly deserve and need. In other words, show them Jesus.

Knowing kids' needs is important if you want to communicate God's truth.

Kids need the gospel

True security, acceptance, guidance, and success can only be gained through a personal relationship with Jesus Christ. God is the only One who can truly meet all of the needs kids may have.

Kids need to know how they can know and love God. They need to continually hear about their need for a Savior.

Help kids understand the gospel and allow God to use you to demonstrate how He will meet each child's needs.

Excerpted from *Bible Teaching for Kids 1st and 2nd Graders*, volume 4, number 2.

Walk-through Tabernacle Replica Reflects Atonement

EILAT, Israel (BP) — As the little girl stepped forward to pull back the ornate curtain, her eyes widened.

"Are we going to die?" she asked.*

She and hundreds of other Jewish children take it seriously when they enter the holy of holies at the tabernacle in Eilat, Israel's southernmost city.

So real to kids

"It's so real to these kids, and interactive," said Josh, who helps with the full-size replica along with his wife Sarah. (Note: Workers at the site have asked that only their first names be used in this article.)

"Children in Israel study the tabernacle in school," Josh noted, "and they bring their tape measures here with them so that they can make sure this one is the size it's supposed to be."

And it is.

The walk-through model of the tabernacle—which gets about 15,000 visitors a year—is made to the stipulations listed in Scripture, Josh said.

"It wows the kids, but it's not just for children, nor just for Jews," said Herb, a missionary living in Israel.

Anything but boring

And to dispel what some might think, he said, it's anything but boring.

"When people read the Bible, they often get to the details of the tabernacle and think, 'Boring!' For many people, it's the driest part to read," Herb said. "But it really is exciting when you get into the details. It lays the foundation for our history of faith."

That's why he and others decided to bring the tabernacle replica to Eilat, Israel from Germany in 2000 — so that people could see that foundation for themselves.

"Without recognizing His dwelling presence in the camp," Herb said of the wilderness account from the Book of Exodus, "how could we understand His dwelling presence in our lives? This is something we need to be able to see."

The tabernacle screams out the message of atonement, Sarah said.

"How many kids in the U.S. have learned about the details of the tabernacle in Sunday School? Not many. But the sacrifices that happened at the tabernacle were the first way God gave His people for atonement," she said.

A picture of reconciliation

The tabernacle replica is a picture of reconciliation in more ways than one, said Yohannus Vogel of the Bible Center, a Bible school in Breckerfeld, Germany.

The German school chose to build the 23-ton tabernacle model to show Israel honor on the occasion of the school's 30th anniversary in 1986, Vogel said. Built on the school's campus, the tabernacle had 15,000 visitors in its first two months. Thirty of them decided to follow Jesus Christ as Savior.

"We prayed and prayed over the project, and it had a great start. Many visitors had an intense response to the tabernacle," Vogel recounted.

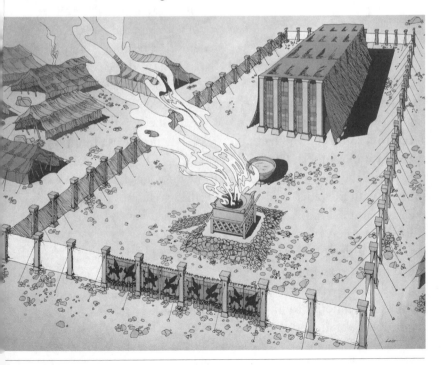

Students manned it and gave tours seven days a week, and some time later the school decided to send it on tour around Germany, Switzerland, and the Netherlands.

"It had 500,000 visitors in all, but afterward it ended up in storage," Vogel said. "We were thinking over it and knew that God hadn't intended for it to end up in boxes."

From Germany to Israel

And that's when he got a call from Herb asking if he could rent the replica and put it in Israel. The same week, Vogel got a call from someone who had space for it in southern Israel, near where the Israelites passed through with the tabernacle on their way to the Promised Land.

"In one week, two people with the same burden of their heart called me in Germany about the same tabernacle," Vogel said. "One had the money to move it but not the land, and the other had the land and not the money."

It was a divine appointment, he said, and in 2000 the tabernacle found its home in Eilat.

It points to Christ

"Our vision for the tabernacle in Eilat is for people to get a vision for the Word of God," Josh said. "We don't want them to think, 'Wow, what a pretty picture,' as much as we want them to think, 'Wow, I want to go read God's Word!'"

As you walk through the details of the tabernacle and see it come to life, the message of redemption becomes vibrant, Sarah said. And the way it points to Christ becomes evident to those who are open to seeing it, she explained.

"When people ask questions, we say, 'Go back and read the Bible for yourselves,'" Sarah said. "If they go home and even open their Bible, that's a huge step."

---

* See Numbers 1:51 and Leviticus 16:2.

Written by Ava Thomas. Reprinted from Baptist Press, *www.baptistpress.com,* © Copyright 2012.